NEWBORNS and PARENTS

Parent-Infant Contact and Newborn Sensory Stimulation

Edited by
VINCENT L. SMERIGLIO
Johns Hopkins University
Baltimore, Maryland

LEA LAWRENCE ERLBAUM ASSOCIATES, PUBLISHERS
1981 Hillsdale, New Jersey

Lawrence Erlbaum Associates, Inc., Publishers
365 Broadway
Hillsdale, New Jersey 07642

Library of Congress Cataloging in Publication Data
Main entry under title:

Newborns and parents.

Bibliography: p.
Includes indexes.
1. Infants (Newborn)—Psychology. 2. Parent and
child. 3. Sensory stimulation. I. Smeriglio,
Vincent L. [DNLM: 1. Infant, Newborn—Congresses.
2. Parent-child relations—Congresses. 3. Physical
stimulation—Congresses. WS 420 N534 1978]
BF720.P37N48 1981   155.4′22   80-29206
ISBN 0-89859-041-8

Printed in the United States of America

Contents

Contributors

Kathryn E. Barnard, R.N., Ph.D., School of Nursing, University of Washington, Seattle, Washington

Richard Q. Bell, Ph.D., Department of Psychology, University of Virginia, Charlottesville, Virginia

T. Berry Brazelton, M.D., Department of Pediatrics, Harvard Medical School, Boston, Massachusetts, *and* Child Development Unit, Children's Hospital Medical Center, Boston, Massachusetts

Evan Charney, M.D., Department of Pediatrics, Sinai Hospital of Baltimore, Baltimore, Maryland, *and* Department of Pediatrics, School of Medicine, Johns Hopkins University, Baltimore, Maryland

Donald A. Cornely, M.D., M.P.H., Department of Maternal and Child Health, School of Hygiene and Public Health, Johns Hopkins University, Baltimore, Maryland

Allen W. Gottfried, Ph.D., Department of Psychology, California State University, Fullerton, Fullerton, California

John W. Kennell, M.D., Department of Pediatrics, Case Western Reserve University School of Medicine, Rainbow Babies and Children's Hospital, Cleveland, Ohio

Anneliese F. Korner, Ph.D., Department of Psychiatry and Behavioral Sciences, Stanford University School of Medicine, Stanford, California

Lewis P. Lipsitt, Ph.D., Department of Psychology, Brown University, Providence, Rhode Island

David R. Pederson, Ph.D., Department of Psychology, University of Western Ontario, London, Ontario, Canada

Marjorie J. Seashore, Ph.D., Department of Sociology, San Francisco State University, San Francisco, California

Vincent L. Smeriglio, Ph.D., Department of Maternal and Child Health, School of Hygiene and Public Health, Johns Hopkins University, Baltimore, Maryland

Mary Anne Trause, Ph.D., Department of Pediatrics, Georgetown University School of Medicine, Washington, D.C., *and* Division of Neonatology, The Fairfax Hospital, Falls Church, Virginia

Emmaline Turner, R.N., M.S., Maternal-Child Health, Department of Nursing, University of Maryland Hospital, Baltimore, Maryland

Raymond K. Yang, Ph.D., Department of Child and Family Development, University of Georgia, Athens, Georgia

Michael W. Yogman, M.D., M.Sc., Department of Pediatrics, Harvard Medical School, Boston, Massachusetts, *and* Child Development Unit, Children's Hospital Medical Center, Boston, Massachusetts

Preface

In present-day hospital settings, some newborns experience early environments in which sensory stimulation is systematically planned and administered. Some newborns and their mothers have earlier and more frequent contact with each other than do other mother–newborn pairs. Some parents are involved in the care of their newborns to a greater extent than are other parents. In short, there is considerable variation in the nature of hospital environments experienced by newborns and their parents. The effects of such experiences are of great interest to researchers concerned with infant development and parent–child relationships, to clinicians involved in the care of newborns and parents, and to parents. This book deals with an analysis of our current state of knowledge regarding the outcomes of such experiences, and with future directions for the study of these effects.

The environmental experiences discussed in this book are grouped into two categories: newborn sensory stimulation by equipment or hospital personnel, and parent–infant contact. The first category includes investigations of several aspects of sensory stimulation, with most of the reported efforts dealing with motion, contact, and auditory stimulation. Measures of effects of these stimulation experiences most often are in terms of infant behaviors and development. Studies in the second category focus on mothers and newborns, and relate primarily to mother–infant bonding and mother–newborn separation. Effects studied include maternal behaviors, maternal attitudes, and indices of infant and child development.

Our present knowledge regarding effects of these environmental experiences is extensive in some respects and yet quite limited in other regards. Although there does exist a sizeable number of research investigations within each of the categories previously noted, these research efforts involve variation in rationale, procedures, study populations, and measures of effects. This variation in combination with other methodological features of the investigations necessitates caution when drawing conclusions about effects. Regardless of such limitations on conclusiveness, decisions regarding environmental experiences must be made in hospitals. More definitive information would be of obvious value for policy making, as well as for a more complete understanding of the underlying processes involved. Although research interest and activity continue to increase, many of the realities of studying these experiential effects create difficulties that perpetuate limitations on conclusiveness.

Contributors to the conference on which this book is based evaluated current knowledge and discussed ways of increasing the quality and efficiency of investigations. Specific issues included the following: choice of modality of sensory stimulation, description of environmental experiences and populations of study, validity of measures of effects, possibility of increased comparability of outcome measures across studies, possibility of coordinating efforts across multiple research groups while at the same time maintaining investigator independence, and the need to deal with factors (such as parental perceptions of environmental interventions, hospital staff involvement, effects of maternal medication) that may influence the extent and interpretation of effects.

The conference was held at Johns Hopkins University. The multidisciplinary profile of the program contributors reflects the multidisciplinary nature of the issues under consideration. Professional fields represented were developmental psychology, nursing (both research and clinical perspectives), pediatrics (likewise both research and clinical views), public health and sociology. Several of the participants are those people most active in investigations of newborn sensory stimulation and mother–infant contact. Several other participants have considerable experience studying infants and parents, but are not directly involved in investigations of sensory stimulation or mother–infant contact. This combination was intended to capture the views of those directly involved and the somewhat more objective perspectives of those less directly involved in these areas.

There are several people I would like to thank for their participation in this endeavor. First of all, I want to express my appreciation to all of the contributors to this book for their considerable efforts: preconference preparation, conference participation, and postconference manuscript revisions. It was highly gratifying to experience the commitment and enthusiasm they demonstrated for the issues and tasks of this project. Special thanks are due to Donald Cornely for the intellectual and resource support he provided throughout all phases of the project. Frank Murray's encouragement and efforts on behalf of the Society for Research in Child Development contributed significantly to the project; his interest and efforts are very much appreciated. I want to thank Ann Koontz and Peggy Parks for chairing sessions at the conference. I was fortunate to have secretarial assistance on this project from the following individuals: Sharon McDonald, Joyce Lyons, and Krista Haley. I acknowledge their contribution with much appreciation. Finally, I want to thank all those unnamed individuals who listened and responded to my ideas regarding the conference and this book.

Vincent L. Smeriglio

This book is based on a conference sponsored by
The Department of Maternal and Child Health,
School of Hygiene and Public Health,
Johns Hopkins University,
and
The Society for Research in Child Development

INTRODUCTION

1 A Time for Taking Perspective

Vincent L. Smeriglio
Johns Hopkins University

In recent years, there has been increased evidence of attempts to understand the effects of environmental experiences which newborns and parents undergo in the hospital setting. Reports in the literatures of several fields (especially developmental psychology, nursing, and pediatrics) have provided information about the effects of sensory stimulation on newborns, usually low-birthweight infants. Several modalities have been employed, including tactile stimulation provided by hospital staff, motion stimulation administered by hospital personnel or by equipment, and differing types of auditory stimulation. Several studies also have been reported on effects of early and extended contact between mothers and newborns. The timing, extent, and specific nature of the contact have varied somewhat from one study to another.

Studies of manipulation of the hospital environment lend themselves to division into two categories based on type of experience: newborn sensory stimulation, and mother–infant contact. As just indicated, within each category the specifics of the environmental manipulations have varied across investigations. In addition, the rationale for intervention has differed somewhat. For example, in some cases the rationale for administering sensory stimulation to premature infants has been to compensate for in utero experiences missed because of early delivery. In other cases, the basis has been to compensate for what is assumed to be a deprived sensory environment in a hospital's premature infant unit, or to make the environment of the premature more similar to that of the full-term newborn. Although there is perhaps less variability in rationale across mother–infant contact studies, variation does exist. Frequently the postulated processes by which environmental manipulations are expected to achieve effects are not specified in published reports.

The populations studied within the sensory stimulation and the mother–infant contact areas have been heterogeneous. Full-term infants, low-birthweight infants, and premature infants (defined by birthweight in some cases, and by gestational age in others) have been studied. Variation in racial groups and in nationality (e.g., Brazil, Canada, Guatemala, Sweden, United States) has been seen across published reports. These are the obvious variations. Associated with these characteristics are unknown differences in such aspects as parental perceptions of infant development, parental perceptions of environmental manipulations, infant-rearing practices, hospital policies, hospital-staff behaviors, and a list of other characteristics quite capable of influencing the effects of environmental manipulations.

The procedures used to assess effects of environmental manipulations have been numerous. Measures have included infant weight gain, infant irritability, crying, sleep patterns, performance on developmental scales, observations of infant and maternal behaviors during feeding, maternal attitudes, and maternal self-confidence ratings. Given the difficulties in assessing the effects of interest, of necessity the measures often lack proven validity.

As the foregoing discussion indicates, investigations of newborn sensory stimulation and mother–infant contact are certainly characterized by variation in rationale for intervention, postulated mechanisms of effect, study populations, and procedures of intervention and assessment. Such variation, of course, is not to be viewed negatively in and of itself. Quite to the contrary, knowledge of how environmental manipulations differentially affect outcomes in relation to identifiable population characteristics is very important information. Similarly, systematic study of effects of components of environmental manipulations can lead to improved effectiveness of future interventions. Working from different rationales in some instances can result in more sophisticated understanding of phenomena. However, in order to benefit from variation in rationale, study population, and intervention specifics, other methodological requirements must be met, such as adequate sample size, complete delineation of sample characteristics and procedures, and some commonality of outcome measures. On the whole, such requirements have not been met in the body of research reporting on newborn sensory stimulation and mother–newborn contact. Very often, the lack of methodological adequacy is a result of practical difficulties (such as obtaining sizeable samples and developing meaningful outcome measures).

Given this situation, it appears that the field would benefit from a systematic perspective-taking analysis of our current state of knowledge. A very important component of this analysis is the consideration of possible ways to accelerate research progress (including ways of dealing with the very real practical difficulties).

The issues set forth by Bell and Hertz (1976) provide one meaningful context for such a perspective-taking analysis. In that article, Bell and Hertz call for attempts at more comparability and generalizability of developmental research in the interest of more rapid establishment of dependable, agreed-upon findings. They focus on two major means of working toward increased comparability and generalizability: efforts toward agreement on critical variables, and efforts at more collaborative research endeavors. In their view, investigators should not limit themselves to studying only the agreed-upon variables, but there should be at least a common core of critical variables studied across investigations on the same topic. Bell and Hertz argue that attempts at agreement on critical variables are most appropriate when there is a quickening of interest in a research area, and yet enough work has occurred in the area to make feasible the attempts at agreement. Debate as to how these considerations relate to newborn sensory stimulation and mother–newborn contact seems worthwhile. Bell and Hertz cite a few precedents for collaborative and semicollaborative efforts, and point out that such projects are consistent with recommendations of some supporting agencies and foundations.

Several of the chapters in this book deal with the ideas put forth by Bell and Hertz. Contributors also consider other issues relevant both to analysis of our present state of knowledge and to directions for future investigations. In Part II of the book, newborn sensory stimulation is viewed from the perspective of comparability, generalizability, and suggested directions for enhancement of our knowledge base. The same is done for mother–infant contact in Part III. Part IV includes considerations of several factors potentially influencing the extent and interpretation of effects in both newborn sensory stimulation and mother–infant contact (e.g., parental perceptions of environmental manipulations, maternal medication and attitudes, interplay of clinical nursing and medical care factors with the environmental manipulations). Part V focuses on issues related to the appropriateness and feasibility of coordinated efforts across research groups. In Part VI, many of the issues of the book are analytically summarized, and specific suggestions are made regarding research design, reporting, and coordination.

REFERENCE

Bell, R. Q., & Hertz, T. W. Toward more comparability and generalizability of developmental research. *Child Development*, 1976, *47*, 6-13.

2 Some Realities Influencing Early-Environment Research

Donald A. Cornely
Johns Hopkins University

It seems appropriate to acknowledge the immense difficulty investigators face in working in the field of infant development. This difficulty is derived from several circumstances:

1. The focus on live births centers on events with which the general public has a very great familiarity. With over three million live births occurring annually in this country across all social and cultural segments of our society, it means the public is not the least timid about discussing and interpreting the observations of scientists surrounding aspects of this event. The public easily recognizes the topic and is very comfortable drawing its own interpretations without the need for the interpretations of the scientists.

2. Scientists quickly find that the constraints and limitations they place on these preliminary findings, observations and tentative conclusions can be rather easily ignored by sizeable segments of society with an interest in childbirth. Speculation by an individual as a legitimate preliminary sequence in the scientific method can very promptly become *fact* to many in society. Bonding and attachment are buzz words among the general public, who wait only to see how long it will take the scientists to ''prove'' what the public is confident it already knows.

3. Public policy on aspects of facilities and personnel involved in assisting in childbirth develops very often without regard to the qualifications scientists place on limited observations. What is manipulated, the manner and attention placed on such manipulations of the environment, and what is posed as the outcome of such manipulation or intervention, all suggest desired ''good.'' Changes in facilities and operating policies become demands from the general public. Re-

7

searchers are not always permitted to assess any possible harm before what is apparent as good is adopted as practice.

These realities do prompt the question of whether we can continue to pretend that we have the luxury of the bench scientist, who deals with more circumscribable and controllable environments in which to examine an endless set of manipulations and seemingly idiosyncratic sets of outcome measures observed on extremely finite population groups. Knowing the ready appeal the newborn-environment topic has for the general public should prompt us to acknowledge that populations under study must demonstrate a greater appreciation of the variations in relevant factors affecting behavior among the three million live births each year.

Random assignment to a study or a control group when dealing with small numbers of 7, or 20, or 30 sets of mother–infant pairs raises questions of the defensibility of study design. We do know that among the three million live births there are many combinations of characteristics in the mothers and infants that impinge on the study question; to allow this host of factors simply to be distributed randomly is both inadequate and inefficient. It will require much larger populations to permit the stratifications necessary to distinguish outcomes between an intervention and a nonintervention group. Hence, there is an urgent need to see if some consensus can be reached on the types of interventions, the methods of measurement of the phenomena at issue, and the critical personal characteristics of the subjects that must be included.

When discussing intervention modalities, one must also raise the questions of doses and length of interventions, in addition to the content of the intervention per se. The question of *too much* must receive as much appropriate attention as *too little*. If the intervention is seen as sufficiently important to make a difference in an important aspect of human development, is it not reasonable to expect that anything so powerful also contains the potential for harm? It would seem important to consider the inclusion of measures to detect undesirable outcomes and not simply use measures implying that low scores mean an insufficient dose and higher scores mean an appropriate dose of intervention. The responsibility to attest to the safety of the intervention applies both to maternal and infant intervention.

Finally, there are terms that have been used as if they were interchangeable, when the differences in the terms they convey are important considerations. Primiparity is not interchangeable with primigravidity. Premature infants include important distinctions between preterm and small for gestational age. Care during the antepartum phase of pregnancy cannot be assumed to be either unimportant or standardized when considering the issue of mother–infant interaction. Collaboration undertaken to facilitate our knowledge of phenomena under consideration should not mean only that standardized study designs and measurements be used over a prescribed period of time. Collaboration is not intended to frustrate innovation, but rather to recognize a responsibility for circumscribing boundaries rather than employing simple extensions of logic, which become sufficiently remote to make it difficult to reconstruct the question at issue.

NEWBORN SENSORY
STIMULATION

3 Intervention with Preterm Infants: Rationale, Aims, and Means

Anneliese F. Korner
Stanford University School of Medicine

RATIONALE FOR INTERVENTION
WITH PRETERM INFANTS

Within the last 20 years, great progress has been made in the medical care of preterm infants, largely due to technological advances in the development of new life-support systems. The field of neonatology has thus decided to intervene dramatically and forcefully to reduce the mortality and morbidity of this group of infants.

There is far less unanimity among behavioral scientists regarding the need or advisability for additional intervention with preterm infants. In practical terms, such intervention is, of course, not a life and death matter, and therefore does not seem as obviously imperative. But quite aside from this, it is felt by some on theoretical grounds that intervention with preterm infants is a useless, futile exercise because the infant's developmental progress is primarily a function of the natural course of brain maturation, which is thought to be impervious to extrauterine experience and environmental stimulation.

Parmelee (1975) recently reviewed the evidence from a large number of studies comparing the development of infants born at term with that of infants born 2–3 months prematurely who had grown to term. The neurophysiological studies reviewed showed that in many aspects there were no significant differences between the two groups, underscoring the idea that extrauterine experience matters not. However, both Dreyfus-Brisac (1966) and Parmelee, Schulte, Akiyama, Wenner, Schultz, and Stern (1968) found that the sleep patterns of preterm infants were more disorganized. There is evidence that the behavior of preterm infants is more obligatory, particularly in the visual sphere (Sigman,

Kopp, Littman, & Parmelee, 1977). Also, the neurological development of preterm infants who had grown to term is characterized by significantly more weak responses than that of full-term infants (Howard, Parmelee, Kopp, & Littman, 1976). Parmelee (1975) concluded from his review that the preterm infant's development was more uneven and less well integrated and that, therefore, these infants were at greater risk for developmental difficulties later on.

What might possibly cause this unevenness in development in preterm infants? There are, of course, the disruptive influences of the many medical complications with which these infants frequently have to cope. However, most of the studies comparing the development of full-term infants with that of preterm babies grown to term preselected infants whose medical course was not marred by major medical complications. There must therefore be other factors that hamper the normal unfolding of these infants' brain maturation. I can think of at least three major areas that involve complicating factors which may hinder the natural course of development. What is more, I would postulate that it might be possible to attenuate the impact of some of these complicating factors through appropriate intervention.

First, when a baby is born prematurely, the infant is forced to cope with vital functions that the maternal organism normally assumes for the fetus. For example, preterm infants are suddenly called upon to regulate their own temperature, to breathe on their own to remain properly oxygenated, to maintain nutritional requirements by food uptake through the gastrointestinal tract, and to cope prematurely with the impact of gravity, to name just a few of the tasks for which these infants are not adequately prepared. In addition, the infant is deprived of the regulatory influences of the maternal biorhythms involving physiologic and motor activity and rest. This deficit of a potential "Zeitgeber" or "rhythm-giver" may very well contribute to the disorganization of the infant's behavior (Dreyfus-Brisac, 1974; Korner, 1979). In general, when an organism is called upon to function at a level for which it is unprepared, its attempts either collapse or it precociously manages to function, but at the expense of tremendous stress. Both occur in the preterm infant's struggle for survival.

A second factor likely to hamper the natural course of the preterm infant's brain maturation is the fact that these babies are deprived of the sensory stimuli and experiences that attend intrauterine life. From an evolutionary point of view, it is reasonable to assume that these sensory experiences are conducive to facilitating the normal growth and development of the infant.

A third factor likely to interfere with the normal course of brain maturation is the very intervention of keeping these babies alive through the creation of a highly artificial, technological environment in which these infants grow to term. Given the necessity of the intensive care environment with all its life-support systems, continuous bright lights and monotonous white noise, the infant is placed in an environment that has alternately been described as one of sensory deprivation (e.g., Hasselmeyer, 1964; Katz, 1971, Neal, 1967) and sensory bombardment (e.g., Korones, 1976; Lucey, 1977). Although nothing is known at this time about how preterm infants deal with either sensory deprivation or sensory overload, we know from studies with older individuals that both under- and over-stimulation have a disruptive and disorganizing effect on the physiological and psychological functioning of the organism (e.g., Frankenhaeuser & Johansson, 1974). One may conclude from the foregoing that the preterm infant may not now be raised in an environment that optimizes the natural course of brain maturation, and that there may be room for improvement of this environment, particularly in the area of providing more patterned stimulation which is not connected with stressful medical procedures.

Given the unavoidable circumstances of the infant having to cope with tasks for which he or she is unprepared, being deprived of the sensory experiences that attend uterine life and having to grow to term in a highly artificial environment, what interventions might be conducive to lightening the infant's burdens and thereby, perhaps, facilitating a more even development? In my view, such intervention should aim at any or all of the following objectives: Whenever possible, it should reduce stress by supporting the infant's struggle in coping with tasks for which it is really unprepared. Intervention might also attempt to provide compensatory stimulation similar in kind to that experienced by the infant in utero. Furthermore, intervention might try to alter the artificial environment in which the infant grows to term, at least within the limits dictated by intensive care. Thus, it may be of some help to provide within this artificial environment some patterned stimulation that is relevant to the state of the infant's neurophysiological development and that contingently reinforces the developing organization of the infant's biorhythms.

ENDS AND MEANS OF INTERVENTION

In recent years, a variety of intervention studies with preterm infants have been undertaken as Cornell and Gottfried's (1976) review on this subject testifies. Too few investigators have made explicit their specific goals of intervention. Some investigators have tried to condition preterm infants, or have provided visual, auditory and social stimulation, all of which are forms of stimulation to which full-term infants are highly responsive and to which preterm infants of various post-conceptional ages *begin* to respond (Katz, 1971; Scarr-Salapatek & Williams, 1973; Siqueland, 1969; Williams & Scarr, 1971; Wright, 1971). Implicitly or explicitly, the goal of these interventions is to *accelerate* the development of preterm infants. Other investigators have chosen to impart types of patterned stimulation that are highly prevalent in utero with the intent to *compensate* for an experiential deficit (Barnard, 1972; Freedman, Boverman, & Freedman, 1966; Korner, 1979; Korner, Kraemer, Haffner, & Cosper, 1975; Neal, 1967). Each of these investigators has used a form of vestibular-proprioceptive or movement stimulation as the main type of patterned stimulation given to preterm infants.

My own goal of intervention is strictly one of compensating for an experiential deficit. This stand grows out of the theoretical conviction that acceleration of development, if indeed possible, may neither be desirable nor long-lasting. As I view development, I believe that it occurs in an orderly sequence of events. Do we know enough about this sequence to intervene in a functionally appropriate way? Before all, does a faster rate of developing certain functions guarantee a higher level of functioning in the long run? Much of the evidence in the literature suggests that it does not.

My goal of intervention is one of primary prevention of a developmental deficit if at all possible. Our goal is to produce an infant that is as clinically and developmentally intact as possible. By intactness, I mean an infant who has grown to term who resembles an infant born at term as much as possible. Fortunately, there is a fairly large body of knowledge on normal newborn behavioral and neurological functioning which provides some guidelines as to how an intact infant should function. There are also a number of assessment procedures available, at least for full-term infants, that can be used to assess outcome, the choice of which should be dictated by a given investigator's goals of intervention. Thus, if one wants to find out whether or not a preterm infant's capability of interaction with his mother and his environment is comparable to that of infants born at term, one would undoubtedly use the Brazelton Neonatal Behavioral Assessment Scale (Brazelton, 1973). Were one to attempt to find out whether the infant had a basic defect in neurological functioning, one would use the Prechtl and Beintema (1964) or the Graham (1956) Examination. The outcome procedures that are probably the most relevant for assessing the effects of intervention are those that test the maturity of the infant's functioning. In this domain, the Amiel-Tison (1968), the Brazelton (1973), the Finnstrom (1971), and the Rosenblith (1961) revision of the Graham Examination are of help. I, for one, would want to know how randomly assigned experimental and control groups of preterm infants differ in the level of maturity of functioning with respect to the infants' sleep organization, the development of active and passive tone, the maturity of the infants' capability to withstand fatigue and ability to display some stamina. I would, of course, also be interested in how these infants differ in their availability to interact with the environment which some of the Brazelton items tap so very well. Thus, my question would address the issue of whether or not the functioning of prematurely born infants from an experimental group approximates more closely the functioning of full-term infants than does that of a control group. If it does, this would suggest that by intervening, we may have created conditions that facilitate a more natural course of the infants' maturation.

What then, are the means that we are using to intervene with preterm infants? For a number of theoretical reasons and based on a great deal of empirical evidence from our earlier studies with human infants and rat pups, all of which pointed to the fundamental importance of movement stimulation for very early development (Gregg, Haffner, & Korner, 1976; Korner & Grobstein, 1966; Korner & Thoman, 1970, 1972; Thoman & Korner, 1971), we have decided to provide vestibular-proprioceptive stimulation to preterm infants in order to compensate for an experiential deficit. In utero, the fetus experiences a great deal of movement stimulation through its continuous flotation in the amniotic fluid, its own movements which are dampened and modulated by the fluid environment, as well as the pattern of the mother's periodic movements. In the incubator, the preterm infant resides on a hard and stationary surface; if ill, the infant moves very little and if not ill, the infant's movements are frequently characterized by an overshooting, jerky quality that reflects the immaturity of the infant's inhibitory mechanisms. When moved by others, this occurs mostly at arbitrary and brief intervals when dictated by medical exigencies. The preterm infant is thus deprived of the quantity, the quality and the rhythmic periodicity of movements normally experienced in utero.

Evidence from the animal literature strongly suggests that the deprivation of movement stimulation may lead to serious developmental deficits. For example, Erway (1975), who works in the area of otolith defects in mice, recently stated that "deficiency of vestibular input, either for reasons of congenital defect or lack of motion stimulation may impair the early development and integrating capacities of the brain, especially that of the cerebellum [p. 20]." Mason's work (1968) with nonhuman primates seems to bear out this statement. Mason, like Harlow (1958), isolation-reared infant monkeys on surrogate mothers. Harlow, as a result of these rearing conditions, produced highly abnormal monkeys who engaged in autistic-like, self-mutilating and self-rocking behavior. Mason, by providing isolation-reared monkeys with *swinging* surrogate mothers, offset the severe developmental deficits and the pathological symptoms typically seen in Harlow's monkeys.

Vestibular-proprioceptive stimulation thus appears to be one of the most important forms of stimulation necessary for the normality of early development. Our means for imparting compensatory vestibular-proprioceptive stimulation to preterm infants is through waterbeds which were developed in our laboratory. I would like to stress that, although the waterbeds create a flotation environment for the premature infant, it was not our aim to simulate intrauterine conditions, for this is neither possible nor necessarily desirable. Instead, we merely want to impart vestibular-proprioceptive stimulation as naturally as possible with some of the formal and temporal characteristics of the movement stimulation that the fetus experiences prenatally. Thus, as will be described later, in addition to providing a flotation environment, we decided to impart movement stimulation that is contingent on the infant's own activity and that, at other times, is superimposed on him in experientially relevant rhythms and intervals.

In developing the waterbeds, we not only wanted to provide compensatory movement stimulation to preterm infants, but we also hoped to ease at least some of the burdens in their struggle to cope with tasks of extrauterine life for which they are as yet not prepared. Thus, by creating a fluid support system, we hoped to preserve the fragile skin of very small preterm infants and possibly to reduce the incidence of intracranial hemorrhages, which can be caused by pressure to the head (Newton & Gooding, 1975; Pape, Armstrong, & Fitzhardinge, 1976). We also hoped to ease the infant's task of having to cope prematurely with the impact of gravity. Although the waterbed does not create complete weightlessness, it does provide a flotation environment that diminishes the impact of gravity to some extent. Further, we hoped through the fluid support of the infant's head, to produce babies who might be aesthetically more appealing to their parents, by diminishing the incidence of narrow or asymmetrically shaped heads, which are so frequently seen in infants born prematurely.

We began the development of our waterbeds back in 1972. Because the levels of vestibular-proprioceptive stimulation that are optimal for development are unknown, we built two versions of the waterbed for use inside the incubator. The basic waterbed provides slight containment for the infant and is highly responsive to each of the infant's movements. The second version is identical in design and consistency, but in addition to the stimulation generated by the infant's own movements, it provides very gentle oscillations.

Because the studies I will report were done with a Stanford-designed waterbed, a description of these beds is in order. The basic waterbed consists of a high-impact styrene shell, a vinyl bag covered by a latex membrane, and a stainless steel frame, which attaches to the top of the shell. The temperature of the waterbed is entirely maintained by the incubator's heating system. When a waterbed is prepared, the vinyl bag is filled with 2¼ gallons of warm tap water treated with algicide and blue dye. The water temperature chosen is 2 degrees above the incubator's environmental temperature, because thermal tests have shown that the water temperature stabilizes at that level. In recent years, we have begun to use the waterbeds with infants who are cared for on open beds with radiant overhead heaters. Because under these conditions the temperature of the waterbed is not maintained by the incubator heater underneath, we have used one-half inch of foam to insulate these critically ill infants from the waterbed. The blue dye in the water is designed to alert the caregiver in the event of a leak which, over the years, has been an extremely rare event. Blue was chosen so as not to be confused with urine, emesis, or blood. Repeated cultures of the water inside the vinyl bag have been negative, even after continuous use for more than a month. Between uses, the waterbeds are readily gas-autoclaved. The frame of the bed provides anchor points to restrain the infants as needed.

In deciding on the kinds of oscillations to be given, I had to address all the issues one typically faces when setting up an experimental study involving stimulation. Direction, rise time, wave form, the frequency and amplitude of oscillations all had to be decided on. In making these decisions, I tried to avoid arbitrary choices as is done most frequently in experimental studies. Instead, I made every effort to make choices that might have some clinical, biological, or experiential relevance.

Considering this aim, I decided on head-to-foot oscillations. This choice was predicated on the studies by Millen and Davies (1946) and by Lee (1954), which suggest that the direction of this motion may benefit the infant's respiratory effort. Because the infant would be exposed to these oscillations on a continuous basis, it was important to make them very gentle. After preliminary clinical observation and input from the medical and nursing staff, we decided on oscillations which measured no more than 2.4 millimeters in amplitude at the surface of the bed, without an infant in place. In order to make these very small oscillations more perceptible to the infant, a wave with a rise time of half a second was chosen. This has the effect of producing a very gentle jolt, which sets the wave in motion, and which is followed by a period of quiescence during which the wave attenuates.

In deciding on the frequency of the oscillations we had, of course, an infinite choice. Rather than making an arbitrary decision, I looked for a biologically relevant rhythm. I felt it was safest to provide a *maternal rhythm* because such a rhythm would probably not interfere with the developing organization of the infant's own biorhythms and would, at the same time, expose the infant to a rhythm to which it would have been exposed, had it not been born prematurely. The rhythm of maternal respirations in the third trimester of pregnancy is such an experientially relevant rhythm. Maternal respirations at that stage of gestation are 16 ± 4 per minute according to Goodlin (1972). I chose the lower rates of this range of frequencies as I felt intuitively these would provide a more peaceful and less restless environment. Between 12 and 14 oscillations per minute were thus chosen. I also felt that the oscillations should occur at slightly irregular intervals, partly to reduce the chance that the infant would habituate and therefore tune out the stimulation, and partly because irregular pulses more nearly resemble maternal respirations.

The following photograph is a more recent version of the waterbed developed for research purposes in collaboration with Narco–Air–Shields, Inc., a company producing equipment for intensive care nurseries. The Air–Shields version of the waterbed has all the stimulus characteristics of the prototype developed in our laboratory, but the design has been considerably streamlined. The new beds are much shallower, permitting more work space in the incubator; the latex membrane has been replaced by a loosely fitting sheet. The anchor points for the restraints are now provided through holes in a plastic flap, which is attached to the sides of the waterbed. The bulb pictured in front of the bed connects to a pneumatic device, which allows the attendant to rigidify and stabilize the waterbed surface for such procedures as lumbar punctures or intubation. We are still experimenting with this feature of the waterbed and may, instead, decide to use lightweight styrene boards, which can be placed in 2 seconds over the edges of the waterbed in case of an emergency procedure.

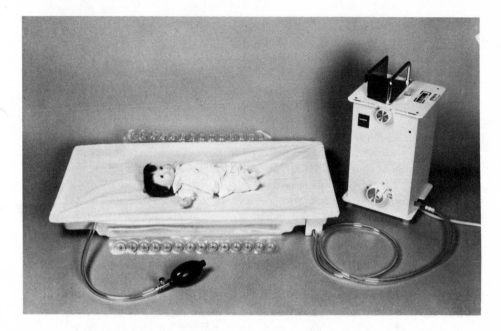

FIG. 3.1.   Oscillating waterbed for preterm infants.

STUDY 1

Because the waterbeds change the infant's environment on a 24-hour basis, a first study was done to ascertain whether using waterbeds in the care of preterm infants was a safe procedure (Korner et al., 1975). Twenty-one relatively healthy preterm infants, ranging in weight from 1050–1920 grams, and gestational ages between 27–34 weeks, were randomly assigned to experimental and control groups. The sample included 10 females and 11 males. The experimental and control groups did not differ significantly from each other in weight or gestational age. The 10 infants in the experimental group were each placed on the gently oscillating waterbed before the 6th postnatal day where they remained for 1 week. The data collected were drawn from the nurses' and physicians' daily progress notes through which the clinical progress of the two groups was compared.

No adverse clinical effects resulted from waterbed flotation. There were no significant differences in any of the vital signs, oxygen requirement, weight changes, or frequency of emesis. We did, however, find one highly significant difference between the two groups: The infants in the experimental group had significantly fewer apneas as indicated by the monitor alarms ($p < .01$). The monitor alarms are set to go off in the Stanford Intensive Care Nurseries when the infant stops breathing for periods of 20 seconds or more, or when the heart rate drops below 100 beats per minute.

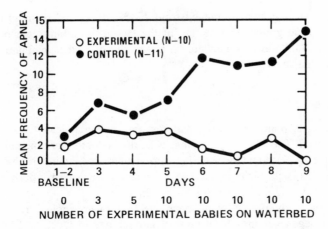

FIG. 3.2 Comparison between experimental and control groups in the mean daily apnea incidence. (From Korner et al., 1975. © 1975, American Academy of Pediatrics.)

Figure 3.2 descriptively compares the mean daily frequency of apnea starting with a baseline average for the first 2 postnatal days. The difference at the start was not significant between the two groups. As can be seen from Fig. 3.2, after the babies in the experimental group were put on the oscillating waterbed, the incidence of their apneas tended to drop, whereas it continued to increase in the control babies.

STUDY 2

Because apnea is thought to be a major cause of brain damage, and because the treatment methods most commonly used are either highly invasive or can cause toxic side effects, we felt that it was very important to replicate our finding. We therefore undertook a polygraphic study to assess the sleep and respiratory patterns of preterm infants who were preselected for having apnea (Korner, Guilleminault, Van den Hoed, & Baldwin, 1978). In this study, each infant served as his or her own control, on and off the oscillating waterbed. This study was done in collaboration with Dr. Christian Guilleminault and his group from the Stanford Sleep Disorder Clinic. Our previous finding was thus tested by independent investigators from a separate laboratory, using more accurate methods of recording and different ways of appraisal.

Sample

The sample consisted of eight apneic preterm infants. We sought to include in this study only infants with true apnea of prematurity by ruling out metabolic, infectious, and cardiopulmonary causes of apnea. Seven of the eight subjects were male. Their gestations ranged from 27–32 weeks and their birthweights from 1077–1650 grams. On the day of the study, the infants' postnatal ages ranged from 7–28 days. None were on any medication other than antibiotics at the time of the study.

Procedure

The infants' sleep and respiratory patterns were polygraphically recorded for a 24-hour period. The 24-hour recordings were divided into four time blocks, with the infant being placed on the waterbed during alternate 6-hour periods. To avoid an order effect, half of the infants were placed on the waterbed during the first 6-hour, half during the second 6-hour block.

Before the study of each infant began, electrodes were applied. Recordings of each child began within half an hour of noon. They included an EEG, EKG, electro-oculogram, and a chin electro-myogram. Respiration was monitored by two mercury-filled strain gauges, one abdominal and one thoracic, and a thermistor positioned in front of each nostril. The infant's behavior was systematically checked by an observer and noted on the record during the entire period of monitoring.

Scoring of the sleep records was done for each 30-second epoch according to the Manual of Standardized Techniques and Criteria for Scoring of States of Sleep and Wakefulness in Newborn Infants (Anders, Emde, & Parmelee, 1971). Because almost all apneas of premature infants occur during sleep, the more an infant sleeps, the more apnea he is apt to have. Therefore, to get the most accurate picture of the incidence of apnea, it is important to assess this incidence proportionately to the duration of the infant's sleep. To this end, an hourly apnea index score was devised. This score gives the number of apnea per sleep hour, or REM sleep hour, etc.

Results

To compute the results, the data from the two periods on the waterbed and the two periods off the waterbed were combined. Two-tailed matched-pairs t-tests were used for statistical analysis.

The results confirmed our previous finding in that apneas were significantly reduced when the infants were on the oscillating waterbed. It was of interest that the longest apneas and those associated with severe bradycardia were reduced the most; periodic breathing or short respiratory pauses were reduced only minimally.

We first compared the incidence of apnea monitor alarms, off and on the oscillating waterbed, as these were the types of apneas that were significantly reduced in our previous study.

As can be seen from Fig. 3.3, apneas were reduced in each of the babies while

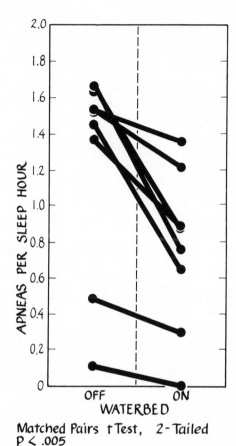

APNEAS PER SLEEP HOUR

OFF   ON
WATERBED

Matched Pairs t Test,   2-Tailed
P < .005

FIG. 3.3. Apnea monitor alarms per sleep hour, off and on the oscillating waterbed. (From Korner et al., 1978. © 1978, American Academy of Pediatrics.)

they were on the oscillating waterbed. The apnea reduction was highly significant, with p < .005.

From the analysis of the polygraphic data, it appeared that reductions of shorter apneas were not quite as marked. The rates per sleep hour of apneas exceeding 10 seconds were reduced in seven out of the eight babies while they were on the oscillating waterbed. These reductions ranged from 13–48%. The most severe types of apneas, as defined by their association with slowing of the heart rate to below 80 beats per minute, were reduced most sharply, at least in seven out of the eight infants. These reductions ranged from 39–60%. Because there was one infant who completely ran counter to the general trend, apnea reduction was significant only at the p < .05 level. Judging from this infant's medical history prior to our study and also after he was discharged from the hospital, this case was probably not one of apnea of prematurity. What was very interesting about this child was that his polygraphic record showed a pattern not unlike that found in older babies who have been identified as "near-miss sudden infant death'' babies for having survived episodes of prolonged cessation of breathing (Guilleminault, Souquet, Ariagno, & Dement, 1976).

In analyzing the polygraphic apnea data, a distinction was made between central, obstructive and mixed apneas. Central apneas are those in which there is neither diaphragmatic movement nor upper airway exchange. In obstructive apnea, there are diaphragmatic movements in which there is no air exchange. In mixed apneas, an obstructive apnea follows a central event.

Of the 873 10-second apneas noted, 92% were central in origin. Average reductions for central, obstructive, and mixed apneas were 25%, 35%, and 29%, respectively. These reductions bordered on statistical significance (p < .08 and p < .10). The results showed that obstructive apneas, which are frequently seen in older babies with "near-miss" episodes, are quite rare in preterm infants, constituting only 3% of the total number of apneas noted in the sample. It is of interest that the apneas of the baby who ran counter to the general trend of reduction of apnea with bradycardia were made up of 20% of obstructive apneas.

In summary then, the two studies we have done so far which used different research designs and different methods of appraisal both pointed to significant reductions in apnea as a function of the oscillating waterbed. One can only speculate about the underlying mechanism that may bring about this effect. One possible explanation is that the continuous, irregular oscillations provide afferent input to the respiratory center and thus abort a number of apneas. Other possible mechanisms of action are currently under investigation. In practical terms, the oscillating waterbed represents a nontoxic, noninvasive method of alleviating a potentially brain-damaging symptom, which affects a large part of the population of preterm infants.

CLINICAL OBSERVATIONS WITH THE NONOSCILLATING WATERBED

As had been anticipated, the waterbeds are very helpful in the care of very small preterm infants who weigh no more than 1 to 2 pounds. The warm bed stabilizes their temperature and the fluid support preserves their fragile skin. The nonoscillating waterbeds have also been found useful in reducing the discomfort of infants with spina bifida, hydrocephalus, disseminated herpes, and other severe skin conditions. In one infant born with blisters all over her body, attending physicians observed that the infant required less sedation when she was placed on the waterbed and from then on, skin breakdown on her back was halted. Further, the nonoscillating waterbed was found useful for infants recovering from abdominal surgery, as these infants could not be turned over, and for infants who were on a regimen of parenteral nutrition because of severe emaciation. We have not yet systematically tested our hypothesis that the waterbeds reduce the incidence of asymmetrically shaped, narrow heads, but this hypothesis has since been confirmed by Kramer and Pierpont (1976).

CONCLUDING REMARKS

Considering the evidence from the experimental studies and the clinical observations we have made so far, it is probably fair to say that in a small way, we have already achieved some of our objectives of intervention in that, to some extent, we are easing the infant's struggle with certain clinical problems. For example, we are supporting the infant's breathing efforts by reducing the number of apneas experienced, and we are thereby reducing the risk of sustaining brain damage through oxygen deprivation. We are also alleviating the stress attending skin breakdown so common in small preterm infants. Although the infants cannot tell us whether they experience less stress on the waterbed, it stands to reason that in any condition in which pressure to the skin or the skeletal structure is painful, comfort would be derived from the fluid support. We have, through the waterbed, reduced the full impact of gravity. Whether or not this conserves the infant's energies, only the sequential assessment of the infant's active and passive tone and his ability to withstand fatigue will reveal. Such an assessment is currently in progress. We have just begun a longitudinal study with critically ill infants to explore further whether or not the waterbed can diminish the severity of some of the clinical problems of these infants and whether the gentle stimulation and the fluid support provided by the waterbed will counteract to some extent the deleterious effects of prolonged immobilization to which infants on respirators are frequently exposed. For example, we are interested in finding out whether infants with severe RDS, with or without apnea, randomly assigned to experimental and control groups, will differ in when they begin to breathe on their own, in their resistance to infections or other complications.

We have as yet no idea whether our intervention has any developmental effects. We are about to begin some developmental studies, using intermittent rather than continuous oscillations. Although the continuous pulses were probably largely responsible for the apnea reduction, for developmental purposes, intermittent stimulation may be far more effective. For example, Denenberg's (1975) review of the animal literature on early stimulation effects revealed that stimulus variation, rather than sensory constancy, is an important, if not indeed necessary condition for adequate development. In search for an experientially relevant rhythm of intermittent stimulation, I again chose a maternal biorhythm to which the infant would have been exposed, had it not been born prematurely. The basic rest–activity cycle (BRAC) as described by Kleitman (1969) is such a maternal rhythm. In the adult, the average length of the cycle is approximately 90 minutes. Evidence is accumulating that the manifestations of the BRAC persist throughout the day and express themselves at night through a cycling of REM and non-REM sleep (e.g., Broughton, 1975; Carskadon & Dement, 1975; Kleitman, 1969; Kripke, 1974; Webb, 1969). From Sterman's research (1967), which points to the strong relationship between maternal sleep stages and intrauterine fetal activity, it appears that maternal cycles exert a regulatory influence on fetal behavior. Clearly, the prematurely born infant is deprived of the potentially organizing influence of maternal cycles (Dreyfus-Brisac, 1974; Korner, 1979). We wonder whether the superimposition of a 90-minute cycle on the infant through oscillating the waterbed for 20–40 minutes within each 90-minute period may not provide an external aide to the infant's own developing rest–activity cycle. Although the idea of superimposing maternal biological rhythms has never been tried with human premature infants, evidence from the animal literature suggests that this may be beneficial. For example, Hofer (1975a) found that rat pups separated from their mothers showed fragmentation in the organization and rhythmicity of their sleep patterns and a reduced cycle length. In another study (Hofer, 1975b), separation from the mother produced behavioral hyperactivity in young rats, which was reduced to the level of non-separated pups by administering experimental stimulation over a variety of sensory pathways with a time patterning similar to the mother's periodic stimulation. Hofer (1975a) concluded from his research that perhaps the "rhythmicity of maternal behavior acts as a Zeitgeber, or rhythm-giver for the infant [p. 153]."

In our first developmental study, which involves preterm infants whose development is not marred by major medical complications, we are testing whether the rhythm of the waterbed oscillations given in a temporal pattern similar to the maternal rhythm of rest and activity has a more organizing effect on the infant's sleep organization and motor behavior than does an arbitrary rhythm involving an equal amount of stimulation. Eventually, we will also study the effects of the intermittently oscillating waterbed on the more long-range motor, neurological, and behavioral development of these healthier infants in order to determine whether changing the premature infant's environment through our intervention facilitates in any way the more natural unfolding of the infant's maturation.

ACKNOWLEDGMENTS

Preparation of this paper was supported by a grant from U.S. Department of Health, Education, and Welfare, Health Services Administration, Bureau of Community Health Services, Division of Maternal and Child Health Research, Grant #MCR-060410-01-0. The research presented here was supported by the William T. Grant Foundation, U.S. Public Health Service Grants HD-08339 and HD-03591, the Boys Town Center for Youth Development at Stanford, and Grant RR-81 from the General Clinical Research Centers Program of the Division of Human Resources, National Institutes of Health.

REFERENCES

Amiel-Tison, C. Neurological evaluation of the maturity of newborn infants. *Archives of Diseases in Childhood,* 1968, *43,* 89–93.

Anders, T., Emde, R. N., & Parmelee, A. H., Jr. (Eds). *A manual of standardized terminology, techniques and criteria for use in scoring states of sleep and wakefulness in newborn infants.* Bethesda, Md.: U.S. Department of Health, Education and Welfare, Public Health Service, National Institutes of Health, 1971.

Barnard, K. E. The effect of stimulation on the duration and amount of sleep and wakefulness in the premature infant. (Doctoral dissertation, University of Washington, 1972). *Dissertation Abstracts International*, 1972, *33*, 2167B. (University Microfilms No. 72-28, 573)

Brazelton, T. B. Neonatal behavioral assessment scale. *Clinics in Developmental Medicine*. Spastics International Medical Publications, Philadelphia: J. B. Lippincott, 1973. (Ms. No. 50)

Broughton, R. Biorhythmic variations in consciousness and psychological functions. *Canadian Psychological Review*, 1975, *16*, 217-239.

Carskadon, M. A., & Dement, W. C. Sleep studies on a 90-minute day. *Electroencephalography and Clinical Neurophysiology*, 1975, *39*, 145-155.

Cornell, E. H., & Gottfried, A. W. Intervention with premature human infants. *Child Development*, 1976, *47*, 32-39.

Denenberg, V. H. Effects of exposure to stressors in early life upon later behavioural and biological processes. In L. Levi (Ed.), *Society, stress and disease: Childhood and adolescence*. New York: Oxford University Press, 1975.

Dreyfus-Brisac, C. The bioelectrical development of the central nervous system during early life. In F. Faulkner (Ed.), *Human development*. Philadelphia: Saunders, 1966.

Dreyfus-Brisac, C. Organization of sleep in prematures: Implications for caretaking. In M. Lewis & L. A. Rosenblum (Eds.), *The effect of the infant on its caregiver*. New York: John Wiley & Sons, 1974.

Erway, L. C. Otolith formation and trace elements: A theory of schizophrenic behavior. *The Journal of Orthomolecular Psychiatry*, 1975, *4*, 16-26.

Finnstrom, O. Studies on maturity in newborn infants III. Neurological examination. *Neuropaediatrie*, 1971, *3*, 72-96.

Frankenhaeuser, M., & Johansson, G. On the psychophysiological consequences of understimulation and over-stimulation. *Reports from the Psychological Laboratories of the University of Stockholm*, 1974. (Supplement 25)

Freedman, D. G., Boverman, H., & Freedman, N. *Effects of kinesthetic stimulation on weight gain and on smiling in premature infants*. Paper presented at the Annual Meeting of the American Orthopsychiatric Association, San Francisco, April 1966.

Goodlin, R. C. *Handbook of obstetrical and gynecological data*. Los Altos, Calif.: Geron-X, 1972.

Graham, F. K. Behavioral differences between normal and traumatized newborns. I. The test procedures. *Psychological Monographs*, 1956, *70*, (Whole No. 20).

Gregg, C. L., Haffner, M. E., & Korner, A. F. The relative efficacy of vestibular-proprioceptive stimulation and the upright position in enhancing visual pursuit in neonates. *Child Development*, 1976, *47*, 309-314.

Guilleminault, C., Souquet, M., Ariagno, R., & Dement, W. C. Abnormal polygraphic findings in near-miss sudden infant death. *Lancet*, 1976, i, 1326-1327.

Harlow, H. The nature of love. *American Psychologist*, 1958, *13*, 673-685.

Hasselmeyer, E. G. The premature neonate's response to handling. *American Nurses Association*, 1964, *11*, 15-24.

Hofer, M. A. Infant separation responses and the maternal role. *Biological Psychiatry*, 1975, *10*, 149-153. (a)

Hofer, M. A. Studies on how early maternal separation produces behavioral change in young rats. *Psychosomatic Medicine*, 1975, *37*, 245-264. (b)

Howard, J., Parmelee, A. H., Jr., Kopp, C. B., & Littman, B. A neurologic comparison of pre-term and full-term infants at term conceptional age. *The Journal of Pediatrics*, 1976, *88*, 995-1002.

Katz, V. Auditory stimulation and developmental behavior of the premature infant. *Nursing Research*, 1971, *20*, 196-201.

Kleitman, N. Basic rest-activity cycle in relation to sleep and wakefulness. In A. Kales (Ed.), *Sleep physiology and pathology: A symposium*. Philadelphia: J. B. Lippincott, 1969.

Korner, A. F. Maternal rhythms and waterbeds: A form of intervention with premature infants. In E. B. Thoman (Ed.), *Origins of the infant's social responsiveness*. Hillsdale, N.J.: Lawrence Erlbaum Associates, 1979.

Korner, A. F., & Grobstein, R. Visual alertness as related to soothing in neonates: Implications for maternal stimulation and early deprivation. *Child Development*, 1966, *37*, 867–876.

Korner, A. F., Guilleminault, C., Van den Hoed, J., & Baldwin, R. Reduction of sleep apnea and bradycardia in pre-term infants on oscillating waterbeds: A controlled polygraphic study. *Pediatrics*, 1978, *61*, 528–533.

Korner, A. F., Kraemer, H. C., Haffner, M. E., & Cosper, L. M. Effects of waterbed flotation on premature infants: A pilot study. *Pediatrics*, 1975, *56*, 361–367.

Korner, A. F., & Thoman, E. B. Visual alertness in neonates as evoked by maternal care. *Journal of Experimental Child Psychology*, 1970, *10*, 67–78.

Korner, A. F., & Thoman, E. B. The relative efficacy of contact and vestibular stimulation on soothing neonates. *Child Development*, 1972, *43*, 443–453.

Korones, S. B. Disturbance in infant's rest. In *69th Ross Conference on Pediatric Research: Iatrogenic problems in neonatal intensive care*, February 1976.

Kramer, L. I., & Pierpont, M. E. Rocking waterbeds and auditory stimuli to enhance growth of preterm infants. *The Journal of Pediatrics*, 1976, *88*, 297–299.

Kripke, D. F. Ultradian rhythms in sleep and wakefulness. In E. D. Weitzman (Ed.), *Advances in sleep research*. New York: Spectrum, 1974.

Lee, H. F. A rocking bed respirator for use with premature infants in incubators. *Journal of Pediatrics*, 1954, *44*, 570–573.

Lucey, J. F. Is intensive care becoming too intensive? *Pediatrics: Neonatology Supplement*, 1977, *59*, 1064–1065.

Mason, W. A. Early social deprivation in the non-human primates: Implications for human behavior in environmental influences. In D. C. Glass (Ed.), *Environmental influences*. New York: Rockefeller University Press & Russell Sage Foundation, 1968.

Millen, R. S., & Davies, J. See-saw resuscitator for the treatment of asphyxia. *American Journal of Obstetrics and Gynecology*, 1946, *52*, 508–509.

Neal, M. V. The relationship between a regimen of vestibular stimulation and the developmental behavior of the premature infant. (Doctoral dissertation, New York University, 1967). *Dissertation Abstracts International*, 1971, (University Microfilm).

Newton, T. H., & Gooding, C. A. Compression of superior sagittal sinus by neonatal calvarial molding. *Radiology*, 1975, *115*, 635–640.

Pape, K. E., Armstrong, D. L., & Fitzhardinge, P. M. Central nervous system pathology associated with mask ventilation in the very low birthweight infant: A new etiology for intracerebellar hemorrhages. *Pediatrics*, 1976, *58*, 473–483.

Parmelee, A. H. Neurophysiological and behavioral organization of premature infants in the first months of life. *Biological Psychiatry*, 1975, *10*, 501–512.

Parmelee, A. H., Schulte, F. J., Akiyama, Y., Wenner, W. H., Schultz, M. A., & Stern, E. Maturation of EEG activity during sleep in premature infants. *Electroencephalography and Clinical Neurophysiology*, 1968, *24*, 319–329.

Prechtl, H. F., & Beintema, D. *The neurological examination of the full-term newborn infant*. Little Club Clinics in Developmental Medicine (No. 12), London: William Heinemann Medical Books, Ltd., 1964.

Rosenblith, J. The modified Graham behavior test for neonates: Test–retest reliability, normative data, and hypotheses for future work. *Biologia Neonatorum*, 1961, *3*, 174–192.

Scarr-Salapatek, S., & Williams, M. L. The effects of early stimulation on low-birth-weight infants. *Child Development*, 1973, *44*, 94–101.

Sigman, M., Kopp, C. B., Littman, B., & Parmelee, A. H. Infant visual attentiveness in relation to birth condition. *Developmental Psychology*, 1977, *13*, 431–437.

Siqueland, E. *Further developments in infant learning*. Symposium on Learning Processes of Human Infants, XIXth International Congress of Psychology, London, 1969.

Sterman, M. B. Relationship of intrauterine fetal activity to maternal sleep stage. *Experimental Neurology*, 1967, *Supplement 4*, 98–106.

Thoman, E. B., & Korner, A. F. Effects of vestibular stimulation on the behavior and development of rats. *Developmental Psychology, 1971, 5,* 92–98.

Webb, W. B. Twenty-four-hour sleep cycling. In A. Kales (Ed.), *Sleep: Physiology and Pathology: A Symposium.* Philadelphia: J. B. Lippincott, 1969.

Williams, M. L., & Scarr, S. Effect of short term intervention on performance in low-birth-weight, disadvantaged children. *Pediatrics, 1971, 47,* 289–298.

Wright, L. The theoretical and research base for a program of early stimulation, care, and training of premature infants. In J. Hellmuth (Ed.), *The exceptional infant: Studies in abnormalities* (Vol. 2). New York: Brunner/Mazel, 1971.

4
A Program of Temporally Patterned Movement and Sound Stimulation for Premature Infants

Kathryn E. Barnard
University of Washington

INTRODUCTION

The impetus for the study of a temporal pattern of movement and sound stimulation for premature infants (Premature Infant Refocus Project) grew out of accumulating evidence about the importance of the early environment in establishing response patterns that had potential significance in the child's mental development. Infants born prematurely are at risk in their progress on the continuum of future human development. Many suffer hazards of potential mental retardation, cerebral palsy, growth failure, birth defects, neurological deficits and cerebral dysfunction (Beargie, James, & Green, 1970; Braine, Heimer, Wortis, Wortis, & Freedman, 1966; Rothschild, 1967; Vandenberg, Stafford, & Brown, 1968). Changes in neonatal intensive care may show results of differing rates of neurological sequelae than older studies (Kopp & Parmelee, 1979). However, the data still suggest a high degree (15–32%) of later neurological dysfunction in the premature population when followed until school age.

Generalized expertise in technological advances now places health care disciplines in a different position to approach care of the premature infant. In the past, there has not been equal attention put toward the *quality* of infant survival. Focusing on the issue of quality of survival, one of the first and most obvious differences between the term infant and the premature is the greater difficulty the latter has adjusting to extrauterine life. The immature infant expresses this difficulty in his degree of respiratory distress, hyperbilirubinemia, temperature instability and weight loss, or slow weight gain. To understand the possible origins of such difficulties, it must be recognized that the premature differs in two rather different ways from his or her full-term brother. First, the premature is in a very different kind of environment for the last weeks or months of the normal gestational period. Second, he or she is physically, particularly neurologically, less mature when forced to face the extrauterine environment.

The appropriate stimulus conditions for supporting the neurological and behavioral organization of the premature infant are not known. Prior research in the care of the premature has primarily been directed at questions of survival. As a result of these past efforts, the survival rate of preterm, low-birthweight infants has dramatically improved; subsequently the quality of postnatal growth and development emerges as a paramount issue. There is overwhelming evidence that the postnatal environment of the infant influences subsequent development. This evidence comes from the National Collaborative Study on Pregnancy and the outcomes of these pregnancies (Broman, Nichols, & Kennedy, 1975; Niswander & Gordon, 1972); the study of children of Kaui (Werner, Bierman, & French, 1971); the Nursing Assessment Study (Barnard & Eyres, 1979); and at least 12 studies in which stimulation was provided to premature infants (Barnard, 1976; Friedman & Vietze, 1972; Hasselmeyer, 1964; Katz, 1971; Korner, Kraemer, Haffner, & Cosper, 1975; Kramer & Pierpont, 1976; Powell, 1974; Scarr-Salapatek & Williams, 1973; Segall, 1972; Solkoff, Yaffe, Weintraub, Blase, 1969; Van den Daele, 1970).

Furthermore, it is becoming evident that quite minor changes in the environment during a sensitive period influence both immediate behaviors and longer term growth, development and behavioral patterns (Korner et al., 1975; Powell, 1974; Smith & Steinschneider, 1975). Stimulation experiments with premature infants have largely been based on the stimulation deficit hypothesis. Therefore, tactile, kinesthetic, auditory, and visual stimuli have been added to the infant's environment in varying amounts and at various periods in the postnatal period. Although there has been wide variation in stimulus modality, in intensity, and in timing, most report positive outcomes in growth or developmental measures. The period of follow-up in most of the studies was limited to the early in-hospital period. The longest follow-up has been made by Scarr-Salapatek and Williams (1973), who studied the infants at 12 months of age, and by Barnard (1976), who had a 1½-year follow-up. Although the positive results have been impressive, and the follow-up supportive, one ponders the advisability of making changes in the early environment of the premature on data from a period of development known for its lack of stability. Most researchers would hesitate to call any developmental testing or interactional data exemplary of more stable conditions until at least the 2nd year of life. Therefore, we have virtually no follow-up of premature infant intervention that deals with the outcomes at a more stable period in development.

ENVIRONMENTAL SUPPORTS

It is in the area of environmental support to the premature infant's developmental progress that the Premature Infant Refocus Project has directed its efforts. The specific concern addressed by the project has been the absence of a temporal patterning of stimulation, which would support the organization and integration of behavior for the preterm infant born prior to 34 weeks of age. The control of behavior, particularly activity and inactivity and sleep–wake behavior before 35 weeks of gestational age, is problematic for the young infant because the central nervous system control that allows for the organization of distinct quiet and active sleep states, and the periodicity of state patterns cannot be controlled intrinsically due to a lack of neurological development. Hence, it has been proposed that there is a need for extrinsic support.

In utero it is believed that the mother's patterns of inactivity/activity and sleep provide the kind of organizing and temporal feedback that the baby could use to organize periods of inactivity and activity (Grimwade, Walker, & Wood, 1970; Rothschild, 1967). The incubator environment as it exists today provides for constant sources of stimulation with regard to light, sound, temperature, and other stimuli that have an irregular occurrence in terms of the baby's own activity pattern and caretaking activities. The ecological niche of the preterm infant must provide at least the essential condition for the proper negotiation of the profound revision after birth in the temporal organization of the infant's various functions (Sander, 1975). In 1974, Condon and Sander proposed the concept of self-synchrony as a very important aspect of learning and of social interaction. It was the concept of the developing coordination and integration of the infant's physiological and behavioral responses toward which the treatments were designed. Specifically, low density, repetitive, auditory, and kinesthetic temporally patterned stimulation programs (Barnard, 1973) were used to determine if the immature infant's ability to suppress activity could be enhanced and, if so, how this influenced maturation and behavioral organization.

DESCRIPTION OF EXPERIMENTAL CONDITIONS

The basic experimental condition, an oscillating bed and heartbeat tone for a 15-minute period, originated from a prior Barnard study (1973). In the Premature Infant Refocus work, the temporal patterning of the stimuli was identified as fixed-interval and self-activated. The fixed-interval schedule provided a type of organization for the infant with the stimuli being given for 15 minutes each hour. The rationale suggested that with exposure to this regular temporal patterning, the infant organized behavior so that he or she has less activity during the periods of stimuli. Furthermore, the repetition, gentle oscillations, and heartbeat tone helped maintain a quiet state. The second temporal pattern was termed self-activated. In this temporal pattern the infant's own motor activity was monitored and the oscillating bed and heartbeat automatically turned on at a time when the infant was inactive. This temporal pattern theoretically supported the emerging organization of the infant by providing the stimulation that promoted behavioral quietness at a time when the infant self-initiated that state rather than becoming entrained to an environmental stimulus that initiated the behavioral quietness.

The fixed-interval and self-activated temporal patterns constituted the planned experimental groups. There was another experimental group that resulted from the switches regulating the temporal patterning having been set, by mistake, to produce a combination of the fixed-interval and self-activated. Therefore, there was a third experimental group called quasi-self-activated. The final group of infants in the study were the control group. This group had no temporally patterned stimulation and had the same medical and nursing care as the treatment groups.

SAMPLE SELECTION

The 128 subjects recruited for the study were either born or transported to the Neonatal Intensive Care Unit (NICU), University of Washington Hospital in Seattle, Washington, from September 1975 through June 1978. There were three factors considered in the recruitment of subjects and in randomized block assignment of subjects to groups: gestational age, infant postnatal health status, and previous caregiving experience of the mother. The study used 16 strata, defined by the three prognostic factors, to assign subjects randomly to each of the original experimental and control groups. The distribution of subjects in the treatment and control groups was: fixed-interval, 37; self-activated, 30; quasi-self-activated, 10; control, 27; dropped, 24. The infants dropped from the study following enrollment were dropped because of early death and/or withdrawal from the study because of transfer back to referring hospital. A final total of 102 subjects was the focus for examining the treatment effects.

The exclusion criteria used in selecting infants were: (1) gestational age > 34 weeks and > 15 days of living age; (2) infants with Down's Syndrome; (3) late pregnancy drug-addicted mothers; (4) known major central nervous system dysfunction (anencephaly); (5) infants who were to be adopted; (6) infants requiring assisted respiration during the first 15 days of hospitalization (the respirator was technically incompatible with the oscillating motion); (7) infants transferred in from selected area hospitals with a history of rapidly resuming care when the infant stabilized.

As most investigators involved with high-risk infant populations can attest, the task of recruiting and selecting subjects is one of the most frustrating in the business. For instance, of approximately 36 infants admitted per month to the University of Washington NICU, 50% or 18 infants met the gestational age criteria. For the 18 infants ≤ 34 weeks of gestational age, six per month were not excluded by other criteria. For these remaining six, 70% or 4.2 subjects a month were actually recruited. Thirty percent were not recruited from those meeting all criteria because parents did not want to give consent (15%) or because of short-stay transfer problems (15%). The amount of staff time needed for recruitment is considerable because all admissions must be reviewed, and then for at least 50% of admissions, parents need to be consulted about the study; if they consent, then further gestational age assessment and chart review is done.

We noticed a definite impact of regionalized perinatal care during the course of the study, in that many more infants were being sent back to the referral hospital as soon as care in the tertiary-care unit had stabilized the infant. This resulted in creating, during the study, exclusion criterion number seven, because a number of infants were being put in the study only to be unexpectedly and swiftly discharged to another hospital within 3–4 days. Neither the treatments nor data collection were possible under transfer circumstances. It should be clear that the subjects studied represent 10–15% of the typical NICU tertiary-care population. The majority represents a group of infants, born between 30–34 weeks of gestational age, who had considerable neonatal adjustment problems (but no known central nervous system dysfunction), and who were their mother's first living child. Our initial decision to use a randomized blocking design in subject assignment to treatment group maximizes our ability to analyze the data by overall groups and by within-stratum single-subject comparisons.

TREATMENT AND DATA COLLECTION PERIOD

In keeping with our notion of the preterm infant's problem of unstable function, we elected to define the treatment period for a variable length of time determined by the infant's need for incubator care. Thus the treatment period began after the subject was recruited, assigned to a group, and baseline data collected; this was generally 24–48 hours after recruitment. Preliminary analysis on 73 subjects revealed the mean number of days of treatment for the three experimental groups was 20.1, and the range was from 8 to 53. Infants in the self-activated group had an average of 6 additional days of treatment. Thus, the interaction between treatment type and amount must be considered in all data analysis.

We chose to deliberately go against the tide in selecting our basis for the times of data collection. The major influence for data collection is the infant's living age, because we consider the bottom line to be how the infant negotiates the revision of temporal organization, functions in extrauterine circumstances, and how this negotiation influences leraning, behavioral organization, and social interaction. Most crucially, we take the position that the infant's present function is a major stimulus for the parent–child interaction and thus has a potentially important influence on that specific social interaction, regardless of whether the behavior is or is not appropriate for gestational age. On standardized measures we can present age-corrected data; however, the data is collected with living age as the reference. We feel this position is justified because the infant's subsequent development is the product of the organism/environment interaction, rather than either alone.

The schedule of data collection for this study is summarized as follows: (1) *Hospital Period*—Baseline at 24–48 hours after recruitment, 4 days later, 8 days later, 12 days later, at 34 weeks gestational age, and at 24 hours prior to discharge; (2) *Post-Discharge Period*—1 month post-discharge, and at 4,8,12,18,24 months living age.

Considering our mean gestational age at birth was 31 weeks, this meant that for every measure standardized on term infants our subjects were examined approximately 2 months prior to the standardization sample's testing. For instance, one measure we used was the Brazelton Neonatal Assessment Scale. We tested the infants at 34 weeks gestational age, just prior to discharge and at 1 month after discharge. We found the infant's performance at discharge was poorer than the term infant's discharge testing. It is important to our prior argument for testing based on living age that although the premature infants showed fewer differences when tested at the same conceptional age as term babies, the premature babies at discharge performed below the term infant's performance at discharge. By 4 weeks of post-discharge, their parents had already had considerable experience with a baby who was less responsive and less well-organized motorically than a full-term infant.

MEASURES

This study was both designed and carried out by investigators representing a number of disciplines; thus it was possible to be more comprehensive in our consideration of dependent measures. Table 4.1 describes the measures and notes the time of collection.

We hypothesized prior to conducting the study that providing the temporally regulated pattern of auditory and kinesthetic sensory input to the infant born prior to 34 weeks gestational age would facilitate (1) organization of sleep–wake behavior; (2) neurological development; (3) behavioral responsiveness; (4) interactive behavior; and (5) parent perception and care-giving. It was further hypothesized that the self-activated group would produce greater change than the fixed-interval group. We hypothesized no differences between the quasi-self-activated group and the fixed-interval and self-activated group.

TABLE 4.1
Description of Dependent Measures

1. Sleep-Wake Activity
   A. Time-lapse video recording of infant's behavior activity for 24-hour periods on all subjects
   B. Polygraphic sleep recording during an intrafeed interval on approximately 1/10 of sample population
   C. Seven-day record mother keeps of sleep-wake activity at 1 month post discharge and 4 and 8 months post birth
2. Neurological, Motor, and Mental Development
   A. Brazelton Neonatal Assessment, Premature adaptation at 34 weeks conceptional age, prior to discharge and 1-month post hospital discharge
   B. Assessment of muscle tone, reflexes, state during hospital period using adaptation of the following schemas: Saint-Anne Dargassies (1969), Prechtl & Beintema (1964), Wenner (1975)
   C. Brain stem evoked responses to auditory stimuli at 4 months post birth (Salamy, McKean, & Buda, 1975; Schulman-Galambos & Galambos, 1975; Weber, 1976
   D. Bayley Scales of Mental, Motor, and Behavioral Development at 8 months and 24 months post birth (Bayley, 1969)
3. Parent-Infant Interaction
   A. Observation and rating of interaction during a teaching and feeding session at 4, 8, and 24 months post birth (Barnard, Wenner, Weber, Gray, & Peterson, 1976)
   B. Video-taping and coding of newborn, 4- and 8-month play parent-infant interaction (Kogan & Gordon, 1975)
   C. Interviews with parents (Gray & Williams, 1975)

RESEARCH QUESTIONS

We were guided in our analysis by the following experimental questions:

Organization of Sleep-Wake Behavior
1. Do the experimental treatments influence the level of motor activity in a 24-hour period?
2. Do the experimental treatments influence the presence of alternating active and quiescent periods in the 24-hour period?
3. Do the experimental treatments influence diurnal patterns of activity?
4. Do the experimental treatments influence the simultaneous occurrence of multiple state-specific patterns of physiological and behavioral activity?

Neurological Development
1. Do the experimental treatments influence the development of muscle tone?
2. Do the experimental treatments influence the development of symmetrical reflex behavior?
3. Do the experimental treatments influence the development of motor behavior?

4. Do the experimental treatments influence state stability during the neonatal period?
5. Do the experimental treatments reduce the latencies of the infant's brain stem evoked responses (BERs)?
6. Do the experimental treatments increase the infant's ability to respond to rapid rates of stimulus presentations?
7. Do the experimental treatments reduce the amount of intra-subject BER latency variability?
8. Do the experimental treatments increase the infant's adaptive sleep-activity pattern through the first 8 months of life?

Behavioral Responsiveness

1. Do the experimental treatments influence the infant's behavioral responses to auditory stimuli?
2. Do the experimental treatments influence the infant's behavioral responsiveness to visual stimuli?
3. Do the experimental treatments influence the infant's responsiveness to the human voice or face?
4. Do the experimental treatments influence the infant's behavioral characteristics as measured by activity level, attention, motivation, and cooperativeness during developmental testing?

Interactive Behavior

1. Do the experimental treatments influence the frequency of codable interactive behaviors in the video-recorded observations just prior to hospital discharge?
2. Do the experimental treatments influence the frequency of contingencies between mother and infant behaviors during the first 24 months?
3. Do the experimental treatments influence the incidence of positive interactive patterns between the mother and infant?
4. Do the experimental treatments influence the occurrence of positive scores on the parent–infant teaching scales? Feeding scales?

Parent Perception and Caregiving

1. Do the experimental treatments influence the parent's perception of the infant?
2. Do the experimental treatments influence the parent's use of supporting resources such as parents' groups, individual contact with other parents, health care services?
3. Do the experimental treatments influence the amount of total caregiving the infant has during the hospital period?

General

1. Do the experimental treatments interact with "family status" variables (e.g., psychosocial assets, demographic information, health and financial conditions) and dependent outcome measures of motor activity; neurological development; responses to sensory stimuli; ability to initiate, sustain, and elicit interactive behavior; and parents' perceptions and caregiving?

2. Do the experimental treatments influence the concordance or discordance of an infant's motor, neurological, activity, and behavioral responsiveness?

RESULTS

Data collection and analysis are still in progress. The final 2-year follow-up data will be finished in June, 1980. The selected results presented are intended to describe the nature of the data available for analysis. No statements confirming or denying the hypotheses are possible to make at this time.

Three major purposes of the discussion of preliminary results are to (1) share information on new methods that may be useful to other investigators; (2) demonstrate the evidence that the stimulation is not harmful; and (3) show data from development assessments at multiple time points. The following data sets are discussed: infant activity patterns collected during hospital phase, clinical data collected during hospital phase, and Bayley Scores.

Infant-Activity Measurement

We adapted a technique used first by Sostek and Anders (1975) using time-lapse video recording to describe the activity status of infants. This technique can be used over a long recording period and does not require the attachment of electrode discs. The equipment used was a Sony model AVC-3260 video camera with a 300-millimeter lens mounted on a tripod and connected to a time-lapse recorder. We have developed a system of recording, coding, and analyzing that allows the examination of infant body activity and caregiving events. The activity measure gives three levels of body movement, the type of caregiving, and a record of the programmed stimulation the infant receives over a 24-hour period. A validation study comparing this method with polygraph sleep recording in prematures has been reported (Fuller, Wenner, & Blackburn, 1978). Table 4.2 displays the output for six infants representing the extreme gestational ages and the two major experimental groups and control group. The observation column refers to the time of data collection (100 = baseline; 200 = 4 days in treatment; 300 = 8 days after treatment started; 400 = 12 days of treatment; 660 = crib taping; a 5 in the third column means the baby was 34 weeks old). Next, the total number of epochs recorded is displayed. Each epoch was equal to 1 minute of

TABLE 4.2

Infant Video Activity Data for Six Infants from the Two Extreme Gestational Age Groups Representing the Control, Fixed-Interval, and Self-Activated Groups

Infants	Obser-vation	Total Epochs	Percentage of Epochs				Caretaking	Number of Periods			Mean Length of Period in Minutes		
			Active	Mixed	Inactive	Stimu-lation		Inactive	Active	Stimu-lation	Inactive	Active	Stimu-lation
Level I (Gestational) age at birth under 30.24 weeks													
Control													
Subject 11	100	1496	20	50	29	—	21	33	27	—	11	8	—
	400	1481	12	47	44	—	13	34	7	—	18	15	—
	660	1434	20	44	35	—	36	19	17	—	20	12	—
Fixed-Interval													
Subject 37	100	1497	9	51	39	—	17	33	6	—	17	16	—
	400	1467	15	52	31	32	14	27	11	28	15	14	15
	660	1469	6	65	25	—	28	19	4	—	13	5	—
Self-Activated													
Subject 42	100	1450	36	58	3	—	17	2	33	—	6	14	—
	400	1451	13	66	18	26	14	20	14	22	11	10	15
	660	1482	13	67	18	—	18	15	7	—	12	17	—
Level IV (gestational) age at birth 32.75–33.99 weeks													
Control													
Subject 14	105	1480	26	51	23	—	7	26	26	—	10	9	—
	400	1509	23	41	34	—	13	29	24	—	15	10	—
	660	1443	17	41	35	—	18	33	14	—	12	9	—
Fixed-Interval													
Subject 29	100	1405	24	47	26	—	9	17	13	—	20	19	—
	300	1458	27	43	27	25	21	24	21	22	12	12	13
	660	611[a]	26	50	23	—	26	13[a]	7[a]	—	8	17	—
Self-Activated													
Subject 19	100	1467	12	63	23	—	10	25	9	—	12	9	—
	205	1492	13	46	41	35	15	32	12	37	17	11	12
	300	1123	18	46	36	47	13	27	11	35	13	6	13
	660	1446	18	48	34	—	19	27	18	—	16	7	—

[a] Approximately 12-hour period = < ½ of previous recordings.

real time. The percentage of epochs in which the infant was coded as having high activity, mixed, or no activity is displayed along with the program stimulation and caretaking occurrences. The final columns give the number of periods and mean length.

The infants included in this display were chosen from the two extreme gestational groups: Level I is all infants who were under 30.24 weeks of gestational age at time of randomization into the study. Level IV infants were 32.75–33.99 weeks of age when randomized. Three subjects, or one cell from the blocking design stratum, were chosen so that for each level there was a control and two experimental treatment subjects. Although no conclusions are possible from examining the six cases, certain trends that pertain to our experimental questions are mentioned.

In examining the percentages of 1-minute epochs that were inactive, it becomes obvious that at least in the younger babies it is important to consider the baseline data when interpreting the later periods because the percentages ranged from 3% to 39%. In four out of six cases, the trend was to increase the percentage of inactive epochs. The one case that showed a decrease also had the highest percentage (39%) at baseline. In the prior Barnard (1973) study, it was also observed that the stimulation influenced less quiet state in infants who already had more to begin with and increased the quiet state in infants with an average or below average amount before treatment. Another way to look at inactivity is the number and length of periods. The number of inactive periods decreased in two of the Level I subjects (#11 and #37) and increased in Subject #42. The mean length of the inactive period increased in #11 and #42 and decreased slightly in Subject #37. In the Level IV subjects, the number of inactive periods increased slightly as did the mean length in subjects #14 and #19. Again, in examining the trends, the infants' variability emphasizes the importance of the baseline data and the crib data that gives a pre–post treatment comparison.

The amount of caretaking was of interest because it too is an important influence on infant state organization. The percentage of epochs where caretaking was taking place demonstrated interesting trends. The younger infants appeared to receive more caretaking time, both at baseline (Level I x̄ = 18%; Level IV x̄ = 9%), and also at the crib measure (Level I x̄ = 27%; Level IV x̄ = 18%). In both age levels, the amount of caretaking time tends to increase, although supposedly the infant is more stable and demands less care with age. A tentative explanation may be in accord with the "old sage" advice of leaving the young premature alone to conserve his energy; yet if that were so, one would expect the Level I babies to be having less caretaking time at baseline. An intriguing possibility is that the caretaker becomes more "attached" to the infant the longer they give care and thus a partial explanation of the caretaking time in the two groups begins to take form.

The amount of treatment time for fixed-interval and self-activated seems related to age in these subjects. In Level I, the fixed-interval produced more total time whereas in Level IV, the self-activated had more total time. This is in accord with the treatment rationale—the older baby would be more likely to maintain inactivity for the 90-second criterion for turning on the stimulation. The number of periods for the fixed-interval should be 24 per 24-hour period. The deviations from this could be a function of under or over recording 24 hours (24 hours = 1440 minute epochs) or the splitting of a stimulation period by the staff turning the mechanism off to start a caretaking procedure during the period, which would then produce two short periods. Although the staff were asked to arrange their activities with the infant so it was not necessary to turn off the rocking and heartbeat tone, this was not always possible. The number of periods for the self-activated condition was influenced primarily by the infant, although the same caretaker influence is possible. The average length of stimulation periods was 15 minutes. This was true for the Level I babies who were later subjects. The 12–13 minute period in Level IV Subjects #19 and #29, earlier subjects, may reflect the improvement in our maintenance of the video recorders, because it was established by our data control technician that the recording and play back speed could vary on the condition of the recorder playback unit.

Infant-Activity Measurement: Activity Cycles

A second method of analysis has been developed to discern cycles of relative rest and activity in 24 hours. From 1-minute coded activity epochs, two moving averages were determined: one brief (10 minutes) and the other long (120 or more minutes). These averages were compared for each minute using the long average as a baseline against which variation in the brief average can be highlighted. Specifically, 1-minute epochs in which the brief average exceeds or is less than the long average by a specified amount are designated as active or quiet, respectively. This specified amount is termed the detection criterion (for detection of relative active or quiet) or noise level (the point at which a signal becomes distinguishable from random variation). Computer programs have been prepared to process and output the information about cycles in a format appropriate for further analysis. For a cycle to occur, the recorded activity must go from one activity state to another and then return to the original.

A number of studies of 18 specially selected 24-hour records have been undertaken to gain an understanding of the way the method developed to identify cycles might influence cycle data. These records were chosen as follows. Three levels of infant activity across the whole 24-hour record were identified: low, medium, and high. Three levels of variability in the amount of movement were identified: low, medium, and high. Two examples of each of the nine combinations of these conditions were selected from 400 24-hour records. The low activity and low variability records were from the 10% of records at the extremes in these conditions; similarly, the medium and high activity and variability records were from the middle or upper 10% of the 400 records.

TABLE 4.3
Overall Mean Cycle Durations in 18 24-hour Records Using
Various Long Window and Detection Criterion Values

Long Window	Detection Criterion	18 Record Mean	Range
120	± 0.1001	57.6 min.	33.1 to 90.8 min.
	± 0.1340	62.5 min.	42.0 to 94.9 min.
240	± 0.1001	65.0 min.	37.7 to 104.4 min.
	± 0.1340	69.4 min.	36.7 to 104 min.
360	± 0.1001	66.4 min.	28.9 to 94.9 min.
	± 0.1340	71.4 min.	29.0 to 100.9 min.

In these 24-hour records the long moving average ("long window") was altered successively from 120 minutes through 240 minutes to 360 minutes. The detection criterion was also altered from ± 0.1001 to ± 0.1340.

Table 4.3 shows the modest effects on mean cycle duration of various long window sizes and detection criteria. There is a change in the mean of less than 10 minutes across the different window sizes and a change of about 5 minutes between the two detection levels. These differences are statistically significant ($p < .05$) but are probably not practically meaningful. For example, for individual 24-hour records, the mean cycle durations have a much greater variation with a range of 55 minutes or more from smallest to largest when any specific long window and detection criteria are used. This leads us to the conclusion that individual record effects are considerably greater than the variations that might accompany the somewhat arbitrary choice of a long window and detection criteria, at least within the limits that we've explored. Or stated alternatively, no matter what window size and detection criterion we select, differences between babies' mean cycle durations will be detectable.

The possibility that the level of infant activity and the amount of variability in that activity over the 24-hour record might systematically influence cycle duration was explored in the 18 records that had been chosen. No statistically significant effect on mean cycle duration of activity level, activity variability, or their interaction was found with six analyses of variance, each exploring one of the possible combinations of window size and detection criteria. To maximize the detection of 30–60 minute cycles we will be using the 120-minute window and the ± 0.1001 detection criterion in the cycle program analysis.

Clinical Data Collected During the Hospital Period

The relationship of the outcome of prematures to the routines employed in nursery care has been emphasized by Lubchenco, Delivoria-Papadopoulos, Butterfield, French, Metcalf, Hix, Danick, Dobbs, Downs, and Freeland (1972). In our project, the use of these routines on the research subjects has been diligently monitored with daily recording of the care provided.

Preliminary analysis of this data suggested the following: The estimate of gestational age obtained by the research project staff showed an expected association with the duration of care in the isolette, the duration of gavage feeding, and the duration of electronic monitoring. All of these durations were longer in more immature infants. These findings are expected because these routines are imposed to compensate for the physiologic immaturity found at younger gestational ages. In contrast, the administration of intravenous fluids and the duration of the use of bililights were not associated with gestational age in less than 34 weeks gestational infants enrolled in this study. Only seven of the 52 infants whose hospital course was evaluated for this report received assisted respiration, reflecting the high neonatal mortality as well as long duration of this assistance in survivors, as infants requiring this more than 15 days after birth were not eligible for this study. The only association of these 'care routine' data with the treatments was a briefer duration of gavage feeding significantly associated with the fixed-interval experimental condition.

We interpret these preliminary findings as showing three things:

1. The experimental interventions do not appear to be detrimental to infants because need for isolette care, electronic monitoring, gavage feeding, IV fluids, and the use of bililights is not increased in infants subjected to experimental conditions.

2. Equal distribution of infant maturity and health status across the treatment conditions is supported by the lack of association of care routines that are imposed to compensate for immaturity or illness with any of the treatment conditions.

3. The determination of gestational age, which has major importance as a blocking variable in the statistical design of this research receives support for its validity in the association of gestational age with care routines that are imposed to compensate for immaturity.

Bayley Scales of Infant Development

The Bayley Mental and Motor Scales were administered at the child's living ages of 8 and 24 months. Table 4.4 presents the Mental Development Index (MDI) scores for 16 subjects at 8 months of age. Clearly the differences in performances as reflected by standardized scores is evident in the child's score using living age compared to adjusted age, which takes into account the prematurity. Although the infants were showing skills expected for their prematurity adjusted age, they were all functioning at least one standard deviation below the mean for their living age. This again represents the conflict the parents experience in the delay in responsiveness and development of skills.

Approximately one-third of our subjects were followed in a premature follow-up clinic at the University's Child Development and Mental Retardation Center. The protocol for the follow-up is scheduled for the evaluations based on

TABLE 4.4
Bayley Infant Development Scales Mean MDI[a] Scores According
to Group and in Relation to Life Age and Adjusted Age

Group[b]	MDI Life Age Score[c]	MDI Adjusted Age Score[d]
Control (6)	82.5 (245.2)	97.3 (180.7)
Fixed-Interval (3)	85.7 (253.7)	126.0 (185.0)
Self-Activated (3)	82.0 (254.0)	117.0 (191.3)
Quasi-Self-Activated (4)	80.7 (242.2)	110.8 (178.8)

[a] MDI = Mental Development Index.
[b] Numbers in parentheses indicate number of cases in each group.
[c] Numbers in parentheses indicate life age in days.
[d] Numbers in parentheses indicate age in days adjusted for degree of prematurity.

conceptional age. Therefore, Bayley testing was done on a few children at 8 and 24 months of living and conceptional ages. In a review of six such cases at the 8-month testing, four out of the six tested higher at the conceptional-based testing age. Therefore the evidence does support the notion that if the research is primar-

TABLE 4.5
Means and Standard Deviations for Age-Adjusted Mental (MDIA)
and Motor (PDIA) Bayley[a] Scores at 8 and 24 Months by Groups

Group	n	MDIA $\bar{x}$	MDIA S.D.	PDIA $\bar{x}$	PDIA S.D.
			8 Months		
Control	26	110.88	22.60	101.73	18.55
Fixed-Interval	22	111.05	14.12	105.32	14.04
Self-Activated	19	106.53	20.16	94.37	15.98
Quasi-Self-Activated	9	104.56	16.82	108.89	19.10
All Infants	76	109.22	18.49	101.98	16.80
			24 Months		
Control	13	102.54	15.10	94.77	16.61
Fixed-Interval	9	112.00	14.75	110.44	14.96
Self-Activated	6	106.33	19.54	99.50	12.79
Quasi-Self-Activated	8	120.12	24.02	104.75	15.42
All Infants	36	109.65	18.36	101.81	15.83

[a] On the 24-month Bayleys, two subjects scored above 150 on the mental test; they were given scores of 151 (next highest score was 131). Both of these subjects are in the quasi-self-activated group. On the 24-month Bayleys, one subject scored below 50 on the motor test and was given a score of 49 (next lowest score was 80). This subject is in the control group. Scores above 150 or below 50 fall outside of the normatively defined range for the Bayley. Such scores may occur as a result of adjusting the MDI and PDI for gestational age.

ily focused on a developmental evaluation of the child, the evaluation based on conceptional age will maximize performance. If, however, the research question is directed toward the question of child-environment interaction, then ideally one would test at both living and conceptional ages. For our research the question of early environmental influences on later development was paramount and hence the decision to monitor the children on the basis of living age.

Table 4.5 presents the Bayley Mental and Motor Scores for both the 8- and 24-month test periods. Although the 24-month testing was less than 50% completed for this analysis, the trends are noteworthy. The total sample (all infants category) means show no change over time; the mental score remained at 109 and the motor score at 101. The pattern in individual groups was not as consistent; for example, in the control and quasi-self-activated groups the motor score declined over the two testings. In the fixed-interval and unrestricted self-activated, the motor index increased. On the mental development index all experimental groups showed increased scores whereas the control group dropped.

For the total sample the difference between mental and motor scores was 8 points. The spread for individual groups showed a slightly differing pattern. At 8 months the difference between mental and motor scores was: control = 9.15, fixed = 5.73, unrestricted self-activated = 12.16, and quasi-self-activated = 4.33. In all but the quasi-self-activated group the mental score was higher. At 24 months, the fixed-interval had the least only a 1.56 point difference.

SUMMARY

The strongest evidence presented, in this report, of the experimental treatments' influence on later development was the decline over time of the Bayley Scores in the control subjects. This decline was not seen in the fixed-interval or restricted groups and only on the motor score for the quasi-self-activated. As more data from the project is analyzed, it will be possible to describe subjects and groups on individual measures as well as to describe individual subjects on multiple measures. The basic hypotheses for the study were directed at the notion that differing early experience at a time of rapid central nervous system development would influence both neurological development and behavioral organization, which in turn would influence the caregiver's responses to the infant.

There is a continuing need to define stimulus properties that influence the preterm infant. Whether the temporal pattern or merely stimulation in and of itself are important determinants we cannot yet answer; however, we should have data to better guide that answer.

We have become convinced of the need to look more carefully at the natural caretaking environment in the intensive care nurseries. Studies should be done in relation to lighting, sound, and caretaking events as they represent macro-environmental patterns experienced by the infant. The recent trend of open field incubators should be carefully studied because the infant has no protection from changing air and sound patterns. The early intensive care of infants during the initial 72 hours should be studied. Do the infants have any nonstimulated periods? An understanding of the proper ecological niche of the developing infant will come with careful study of the premature infant's early development.

ACKNOWLEDGMENTS

The author wishes to acknowledge the co-investigators on this project, Carol Gray, Ph.D.; Waldemar Wenner, M.D.; Kate Kogan, Ph.D.; Bruce Weber, Ph.D.; and Art Peterson, Ph.D. They contributed to the overall design of the project and were responsible for individual aspects of data collected. The project was supported by the Maternal and Child Health and Crippled Children's Services, Health Services and Mental Health Administration, University of Washington, Seattle, Washington, grant number MC-R-530348-01.

REFERENCES

Barnard, K. E. The effect of stimulation on the sleep behavior of the premature infant. *Communicating Nursing Research*, 1973, *6*, 12–40.

Barnard, K. E. *A program of stimulation for infants born prematurely*. Paper presented at biannual meeting of the Society for Research in Child Development, Philadelphia, Pa, 1973. (*ERIC Document Reproduction Service* RD 112 544)

Barnard, K., & Eyres, S. *Child health assessment: Part II, The first year of life*. Division of Nursing, Health Resources Administration, Government Printing Office, 1979.

Barnard, K., Wenner, W., Weber, B., Gray, C., & Peterson, A. *Progress report on premature infant Refocus project*. Unpublished manuscript, University of Washington, 1976.

Bayley, N. *Bayley Scales of Infant Development*. New York: The Psychological Corporation, 1969.

Beargie, R. A., James, V. L., & Greene, T. W. Growth and development of small-for-date newborns. *Pediatric Clinics of North America*, 1970, *17*, 159–167.

Braine, M., Heimer, S., Wortis, H., & Freedman, A. M. Factors associated with impairment of the early development of prematures. *Monographs of the Society for Research in Child Development*, 1966, *31*, (Serial No. 106).

Broman, S. H., Nichols, P. L., & Kennedy, W. A. *Preschool IQ: Prenatal and early developmental correlates*. Hillsdale, N.J.: Lawrence Erlbaum Associates, 1975.

Condon, W. S., & Sander, L. W. Synchrony demonstrated between movements of the neonate and adult speech. *Child Development*, 1974, *45*, 456–462.

Friedman, S., & Vietze, P. M. The competent infant. *Peabody Journal of Education*, 1972.

Fuller, P. W., Wenner, W. H., & 8lackburn, S. Comparison between time-lapse video recordings of behavior and polygraphic state determinations in premature infants. *Psychophysiology*, 1978, *15*, 121–127.

Gray, C., & Williams, K. *Premature infant Refocus grant proposal and progress report*. Unpublished manuscript. University of Washington, 1975.

Grimwade, J. C., Walker, D. W., & Wood, C. Sensory stimulation of the human fetus. *Australian Journal of Mental Retardation*, 1970, *2*, 63.

Hasselmeyer, E. Handling and premature infant behavior. (Doctoral dissertation, New York University, 1963). *Dissertation Abstracts International*, 1964, *24*, No. 7–8, 2874.

Katz, V. Auditory stimulation and developmental behavior of the premature infant. *Nursing Research,* 1971, *20,* 196–201.

Kogan, K. L. & Gordon, B. Interpersonal behavior constructs: A revised approach to defining dyadic interaction styles. *Psychological Reports,* 1975, *36,* 24.

Kopp, C. B. & Parmelee, A. H. Prenatal and perinatal influences on infant behavior. In J. B. Osofsky (Ed.), *Handbook of infant development.* New York: John Wiley & Sons, 1979.

Korner, A., Kraemer, H. C., Haffner, M. E., & Cosper, L. M. Effects of waterbed flotation on premature infants: A pilot study. *Pediatrics,* 1975, *56,* 361–367.

Kramer, L., & Pierpont, M. Rocking waterbeds and auditory stimuli to enhance growth of preterm infants. *Journal of Pediatrics,* 1976, *88,* 297–299.

Lubchenco, L. O., Delivoria-Papadopoulos, M., Butterfield, L. J., French, J. H., Metcalf, D., Hix, I.E., Danick, J., Dobbs, J., Downs, M., & Freedland, E. Long-term follow-up nursery routines. *Journal of Pediatrics,* 1972, *80,* 501–508.

Niswander, K. R., & Gordon, M. (Eds.) *The collaborative perinatal study of the National Institute of Neurological Diseases and Stroke: The women and their pregnancies.* Philadelphia: W. B. Sunders Co., 1972.

Powell, L. F. The effect of extra stimulation and maternal involvement on the development of low-birth-weight infants and on maternal behavior. *Child Development,* 1974, *45,* 106–113.

Prechtl, H., & Beintema, B. *The neurological examination of the full-term newborn infant.* London: Spastics International Medical Publications, 1964.

Rothschild, B. F. Incubator isolation as a possible contributing factor to the high incidence of emotional disturbance among prematurely born infants. *Journal of Genetic Psychology,* 1967, *110,* 287–304.

Saint-Anne Dargassies, S. Neurological maturation of the premature infant of 28–41 weeks gestational age. In F. Falkner (Ed.), *Human development.* Philadelphia: W. B. Sunders, 1969.

Salamy, A., McKean, C. M., & Buda, F. B. Maturational changes in auditory transmission as reflected in human brainstem potentials. *Brain Research,* 1975, *96,* 361.

Sander, L. W. Primary prevention and some aspects of temporal organization in early infant-caretaker interaction. In F. Rexford, L. Sander, & T. Shapiro (Eds.), *Infant psychiatry: A new synthesis.* New Haven: Yale University Press, 1975.

Scarr-Salapatek, S., & Williams, M. L. The effects of early stimulation on low-birth-weight infants. *Child Development,* 1973, *44,* 94–101.

Schulman-Galambos, C., & Galambos, R. Brainstem auditory evoked responses in premature infants. *Journal of Speech and Hearing Research,* 1975, *18,* 456.

Segall, M. E. Cardiac responsivity of auditory stimulation in premature infants. *Nursing Research,* 1972, *21,* 15–19.

Smith, C. R., & Steinschneider, A. Differential effects of prenatal rhythmical stimulation on neonatal arousal states. *Child Development,* 1975, *46,* 574–578.

Solkoff, N., Yaffe, S., Weintraub, D., & Blase, B. Effects of handling on the subsequent development of premature infants. *Developmental Psychology,* 1969, *1,* 765–768.

Sostek, A. M., & Anders, T. F. Effects of varying laboratory conditions on behavioral-state organization in two- and eight-week-old infants. *Child Development,* 1975, *46,* 871–878.

Vandenberg, S. G., Stafford, R. E., & Brown, A. M. The Louisville twin study in progress. In S. G. Vandenberg (Ed.), *Human behavioral genetics.* Baltimore: Johns Hopkins University Press, 1968.

Van den Daele, L. P. Modification of infant state by treatment in a rockerbox. *Journal of Psychology,* 1970, *74,* 161–165.

Weber, B. *Premature infant Refocus grant proposal and progress report.* Unpublished manuscript, University of Washington, 1976.

Wenner, W. *Premature infant Refocus proposal.* Unpublished manuscript, University of Washington, 1975.

Werner, E. E., Bierman, J. M., & French, F. E. *The children of Kauai: A longitudinal study from the prenatal period to age ten.* Honolulu: University of Hawaii Press, 1971.

5

The Influence of Perinatal Complications: A Discussion of the Papers by Korner and Barnard

David R. Pederson
University of Western Ontario

Given the theme and location of this conference, I think it is appropriate that we recall the "Baltimore study" on the sequelae of low birthweight (Harper & Wiener, 1965; Knobloch, Rider, Harper & Pasamamick, 1956; Wiener, 1968; Wiener, Rider, Oppel, Fischer, & Harper, 1965; Wiener, Rider, Oppel, & Harper, 1968). This study was a major longitudinal investigation involving an initial sample of 500 low-birthweight infants ($\leq$ 2500g) carefully matched to a group of full-term infants for race, season of birth, parity, hospital of birth, and socioeconomic class. One conclusion from this study is that there is something about low birthweight that is associated with a small but stable deficit in performance on standardized IQ tests. Harper, Fischer, and Rider (1959) reported a mean Stanford Binet IQ of 94.4 for the low birthweight compared with 100.6 for the control group when tested at preschool age. Wiener et al. (1965) found a similar Stanford Binet IQ score difference at the 6–7 year examination (low-birthweight IQ = 92.2; control IQ = 95.7). These differences were still present at the 8–10 year exam (low-birthweight IQ = 89.8; control IQ = 94.7 [Wiener et al. 1968]), and at the 11–12 year exam (Wiener, 1968).

A second major conclusion from the Baltimore study is more disturbing. There appears to be a rather major incidence of academic difficulty associated with low birthweight. For example, Wiener (1968) reported that by sixth grade 55% of the small low-birthweight ($\leq$ 1500g), 43% of the large low-birthweight ($>$ 1500g but $\leq$ 2500g), and 28% of the full-birthweight children were behind at least one grade in school. These conclusions from the Baltimore study are clearly representative of conclusions from the large research literature on the correlates of low birthweight (see Caputo & Mandell, 1970, for a review).

There are two observations that I would like to make about these findings. First, although there are obvious dramatic changes in perinatal care since 1952 when the infants in the Baltimore study were born, the basic findings of a small but stable IQ deficit and a large deficit in school performance still appear. Thompson and Reynolds (1977a, 1977b) have reviewed studies examining the influence of neonatal intensive care therapy. They reported that the neonatal intensive care units (NICUs) have cut in half the risk of neonatal mortality in high-risk populations; among the survivors there is also a reduction of the frequency of severe mental retardation, cerebral palsy, and other major disabling handicaps. As they note, there are very few follow-up studies on the academic performance of low-birthweight infants born since the introduction of NICUs. Fitzhardinge and Steven (1972) followed small-for-date infants who were born between 1960 and 1966 at the Royal Victoria Hospital in Montreal. All the infants were at least 38 weeks of gestational age at birth and had birth weights of less than 2300g. A comparison group was obtained by selecting a same sex sibling who had a normal birth history. When tested at 8 years of age, the IQ scores were lower for the small babies than the controls (97 versus 104). As in earlier studies, the IQ differences were not large; however school performance was adversely affected. Half of the children in the study group were either failing in regular classwork or were placed in special classes, compared with 5% of the control group children.

Similar results were reported by Rubin, Rosenblatt, and Balow (1973). Infants in their study were born at the University of Minnesota Hospitals in the early 1960s. At age 7, there was a small difference in IQ scores between low-birthweight and full-birthweight children (97 versus 102). The low-birthweight children were one-half year behind in reading achievement and had a much higher rate of academic difficulties.

A second observation that I would like to make is that studies looking at other perinatal insults do not appear to show similar long-term deficits (see Gottfried, 1973; Sameroff & Chandler, 1975 for reviews). This pattern of findings is at least part of the mystery we are trying to unravel at these meetings.

It seems to me that there are three general hypotheses that have been offered to account for these findings: (1) there is something physically or neurologically wrong with the low-birthweight infant; (2) there is something weird or artificial about the early environment of the low-birthweight infant; or (3) low birthweight is a marker that in some way disrupts parenting. Because issues relevant to the third hypothesis are extensively considered in Part III, I will focus on the first two hypotheses. One obvious way of testing the hypothesis that there is something wrong with the infant is to use various indices of perinatal stress as predictors of subsequent outcome measures. Parmelee, Kopp, and Sigman (1976) have developed an assessment technique for the selection of infants at risk. Previous attempts at developing long-term predictions from the assessment of perinatal risk have not been successful unless the neurological deficits are major (Broman, Nichols, & Kennedy, 1975; Pape, Bunicic, Ashby, & Fitzhardinge, 1978; Werner, Honzik, & Smith, 1968). As Sameroff has pointed out so forcefully in a number of papers, (Sameroff, 1975; Sameroff & Chandler, 1975), the simple linear prediction from observed early complications ignores the complex trans-anctions between the developing infant and its changing environment.

I have always been impressed with Anneliese Korner's ability to do elegant research by focusing on one or two crucial variables. She has demonstrated that skill again by her attention to apnea. Although the low-birthweight infant has difficulty controlling a variety of functions, the regulation of respiration is of special concern (e.g., Field, Hallock, Ting, Dempsey, Dabiri, & Shuman, 1978; Pape et al., 1978). Thus Korner takes as a given that the low-birthweight infant has major deficits. For her the goal of intervention is to enable the low-birthweight infant to function more like a normal full-birthweight infant. Both Korner and Barnard agree that the low-birthweight infant needs assistance in establishing biological rhythms. For both investigators the goal of intervention is to normalize the functioning of the low-birthweight infant. This goal leads to obvious choices for outcome measures because a lot is known about the abilities of normal infants and the deficits of low-birthweight infants. Korner has focused on respiration patterns. Barnard has opted for a much more comprehensive assessment package.

The choice of a particular form of intervention under this approach is not as obvious. I think the choice of vestibular stimulation is a wise one. The low-birthweight infant is obviously bombarded with auditory and visual stimulation in the NICU, but may lack movement stimulation. Vestibular stimulation is effective in controlling state (Korner & Thoman, 1972; Pederson & ter Vrugt, 1973), and waterbed flotation has clinical advantages in terms of skin care and the possible prevention of intracranial hemorrhaging (Kramer & Pierpont, 1976). Korner has demonstrated that stimulation on the waterbed decreases the fre-quency of severe apnea-one step in "normalizing" the neurological organization of the low-birthweight infant.

The second hypothesis about the long-term effects of low-birthweight is the weird-environment hypothesis. Korner has pointed to the artificial environment of the NICU. Obvious aspects of the environment that are artificial are the lack of movement stimulation and the absence of cyclical patterns of stimulation to support the development of biological rhythms. The provision of 20 to 40 min-utes of stimulation in 90-minute cycles discussed by Korner and Barnard are forms of intervention programs that directly follow from this hypothesis.

Barnard proposes that an additional aspect of weirdness is that the environ-ment is not responsive to the infant's instrumental activities. She suggests that an appropriate intervention is her self-activated stimulation program. Although this idea is sound, I have doubts about the choice of her particular form of infant control. Learning to inhibit movement is not a very easy form of learning for anyone. I would guess it would be impossible for a low-birthweight infant.

As in the case of the first hypothesis, the goal of an intervention program under the artificial-environment hypothesis appears to be to make the functioning of the low-birthweight infant match that of the normal infant. The assessment package that Barnard has outlined is certainly impressive in scope.

A consideration of the artificial-environment hypothesis raises some issues about directions for future research. Many research programs have been devoted to describing the physical and psychological characteristics of low-birthweight infants. In contrast, there has not been much systematic attention to a description of the ecology of the NICU. What is needed is a more complete description of the physical and social environment that the low-birthweight infant is attempting to adjust to. An example of the kind of study that needs to be conducted is the work of Lawson, Daum, and Turkewitz (1977). They provided a description of the physical setting in terms of speech and nonspeech sounds inside and outside the nursery, illumination, and the frequency of handling. The picture they report is a rather noisy, unpatterned environment with lots of speech sounds but much of it outside the nursery. There was little evidence of a clear diurnal cycle. Klaus Minde (Minde, Ford, Celhoffer, & Boukydis, 1975) at the Hospital for Sick Children in Toronto has conducted a similar study except that he focused on the social context of the infant's 6-week period of hospitalization. He found an extreme lack of stability in who was caring for the infant. I believe that a major contribution of Barnard's research program is the development of a comprehensive assessment package. This aspect of her endeavor will add valuable information about the early social environment of the low-birthweight infant.

Obviously, the more that is known about the nature of the infant's environment, the more reasonable it will be to suggest changes in the environment. In the Korner and Barnard papers, there appears to be general agreement about the nature and goals of intervention. In addition to the excellent stimulation programs developed by these two investigators, future research should provide more details about the physical and social environment of the low-birthweight infant.

REFERENCES

Broman, S. H., Nichols, P. L., & Kennedy, W. A. *Preschool IQ: Prenatal and early developmental correlates.* New York: John Wiley, 1975.

Caputo, D. V., & Mandell, W. Consequences of low birth weight. *Developmental Psychology,* 1970, *3,* 363–383.

Field, T., Hallock, N., Ting, G., Dempsey, J., Dabiri, C., & Shuman, H. H. A first-year follow-up of high-risk infants: Formulating a cumulative risk index. *Child Development,* 1978, *49,* 119–131.

Fitzhardinge, P. M., & Steven, E. M. The small-for-date infant: II. Neurological and intellectual sequelae. *Pediatrics,* 1972, *56,* 50–57.

Gottfried, A. W. Intellectual consequences of perinatal anoxia. *Psychological Bulletin,* 1973, *80,* 231–242.

Harper, P. A., Fischer, L. K., & Rider, R. V. Neurological and intellectual status of prematures at three to five years of age. *Journal of Pediatrics,* 1959, *55,* 679–690.

Harper, R. A., & Wiener, G. Sequelae of low birth weight. *Annual Review of Medicine,* 1965, *16,* 405–420.

Knobloch, H., Rider, R., Harper, P., & Pasamanick, B. Neuropsychiatric sequelae of prematurity. *Journal of the American Medical Association,* 1956, *161,* 581–585.

Korner, A. F., & Thoman, E. B. The relative efficacy of contact and vestibular-proprioceptive stimulation in soothing neonates. *Child Development,* 1972, *43,* 443–453.

Kramer, L. I., & Pierpont, M. E. Rocking waterbeds and auditory stimuli to enhance growth of preterm infants. *The Journal of Pediatrics,* 1976, *88,* 297–299.

Lawson, K., Daum, C., & Turkewitz, G. Environmental characteristics of a neonatal intensive care unit. *Child Development,* 1977, *48,* 1633–1639.

Minde, K., Ford, L., Celhoffer, B., & Boukydis, M. Interactions of mothers and nurses with premature infants. *Canadian Medical Association Journal,* 1975, *113,* 741–745.

Pape, K. E., Buncic, R. J., Ashby, S., & Fitzhardinge, P. M. The status at two years of low-birth-weight infants born in 1974 with birth weights less than 1001 gm. *Journal of Pediatrics,* 1978, *92,* 253–260.

Parmelee, A. H., Kopp, C. B., & Sigman, M. Selection of developmental assessment techniques for infants at risk. *Merrill-Palmer Quarterly,* 1976, *22,* 177–199.

Pederson, D. R., & ter Vrugt, D. The influence of amplitude and frequency of vestibular stimulation on the activity of two-month-old infants. *Child Development,* 1973, *44,* 122–128.

Rubin, R. A., Rosenblatt, C., & Balow. Psychological and educational sequelae of prematurity. *Pediatrics,* 1973, *52,* 352–363.

Sameroff, A. J. Early influences on development: Fact or fancy? *Merrill-Palmer Quarterly,* 1975, *21,* 267–294.

Sameroff, A. J., & Chandler, M. J. Reproductive risk and the continuum of caretaking casualty. In F. D. Horowitz (Ed.), *Review of Child Development Research* (Vol. 4). Chicago: University of Chicago Press, 1975.

Thompson, T., & Reynolds, J. The results of intensive care therapy for neonates. *Journal of Perinatal Medicine,* 1977, *5,* 59–75.(a)

Thompson, T., & Reynolds, J. The results of intensive care therapy for neonates with respiratory distress syndrome. *Journal of Perinatal Medicine,* 1977, *5,* 149–171.(b)

Werner, E. E., Honzik, M., & Smith, R. Prediction of intelligence and achievement at ten years from twenty months pediatric and psychologic examinations. *Child Development,* 1968, *39,* 1063–1075.

Wiener, G. Scholastic achievement at age 12–13 of prematurely born infants. *Journal of Special Education,* 1968, *2,* 237–250.

Wiener, G., Rider, R. V., Oppel, W. C., Fischer, L. K., & Harper, P. A. Correlates of low birth weight: Psychological status at 6–7 years of age. *Pediatrics,* 1965, *35,* 434–444.

Wiener, G., Rider, R. V., Oppel, W. C., & Harper, P. A. Correlates of low birth weight: Psychological status at 8–10 years of age. *Pediatric Research,* 1968, *2,* 110–118.

6

Environmental Manipulations in the Neonatal Period and Assessment of Their Effects

Allen W. Gottfried
California State University, Fullerton

This chapter focuses on three general issues. The first concerns the long-term effects of intervention with premature neonates; the second deals with the type of stimulation that seems most promising in terms of effectiveness; and the third involves the comparability and generalizability of results of intervention programs with premature infants.

Since the early 1960s, there have been extensive changes in the medical management of the premature infant during the neonatal period. Most modern centers have eliminated factors now known to be harmful to the premature's development; these include excessive use of oxygen, inadequate postnatal nutrition, and hyperbilirubinemia. Prospective studies on prematures born in the last decade suggest a brighter prognosis for these infants. Neonatal mortality has decreased, and in addition, there has been a marked reduction in the incidence of major neurobiological abnormalities, retrolental fibroplasia, and seizures. Although there has been a pronounced decrease in neonatal morbidity, deficits in cognitive functioning persist as a major problem in the development of prematures. There are continuing reports of deficits in IQ scores, academic achievement, perceptual-motor functioning, and lags in language development. Thus, although substantial gains have been made regarding the physical and neurological status of the premature, there is still a pressing need to improve the cognitive status of these infants.

It has been generally thought that the premature's cognitive impairment was due to brain damage. More recently, investigators have argued that the environment in which the premature spends his or her early weeks is atypical or artificial in many respects and perhaps not conducive to optimal development. In the past 15 years there has been a variety of environmental enrichment programs aimed at ameliorating the developmental status of prematures, all of which have put forth evidence of positive short-term effects of one sort or another.

With respect to all intervention programs, there have been two recurrent major issues. One concerns the problem of whether subjects in intervention programs continue to improve or at least maintain their gains as long as the programs are in effect. The second deals with whether there are long-term beneficial effects of intervention that are exhibited beyond termination of the program. With regard to intervention programs for prematures, there is a critical issue that needs to be resolved; namely, is the neonatal intensive care unit the place to begin intervention in order to obtain long-term and maximal effects? The literature sheds no light on this issue. The vast majority of interventions have been confined to the neonatal period in the hospitals, and all have reported beneficial effects. However, in a recent study by Rice (1977), intervention began only in the first month post-hospital discharge, and here too there were positive effects on weight gain, neurological and sensorimotor development. The Scarr-Salapatek and Williams study (1972,1973) is the only study where intervention took place both in the nursery and at home up to age 1 year. Again, there was evidence of beneficial developmental effects. Although all these investigators report positive results, the relative efficacy of these different programs cannot be determined due to differences in the nature of intervention, methodological design, and assessment measures. The question remains as to whether intervention with prematures must incorporate the neonatal period. Is this a critical period, such that intervention, if modified or intensified, is sufficient to overcome the adverse effects of prematurity? Is it a time when intervention must be initiated in order to obtain maximal effectiveness? Alternatively, is intervention in the neonatal period necessary at all? That is, can comparable effectiveness be obtained if intervention is home-based? If there is no difference in developmental outcome between hospital and home-based programs, then when and where is it more practical and convenient to intervene? These questions need to be answered, and I hope they serve to stimulate discussion and research.

There has been a wide variety of approaches employed to stimulate premature infants. Types of stimulation have included handling, rocking, sounds, and mobiles. I concur with Drs. Korner and Barnard that the most promising types of stimulation in terms of ameliorating and enhancing development in young infants would come under the rubric of kinesthetic-vestibular or motion stimulation. In my view, emphasis should be placed on this type of stimulation, but not necessarily for the following reasons that have been suggested in the literature: (1) that it compensates for experience the infant would have had if still in utero; (2) because it simulates conditions of the uterus; (3) that it overcomes the sensory deprivation assumed to be characteristic of intensive care units; and (4) that it makes the environment more comparable to that of full-term infants.

Although the concept of compensation may serve as a heuristic, it does not facilitate interpretation. Compensating for kinesthetic-vestibular stimulation the infant would have had if it remained in utero certainly appears to improve the developmental status of the premature neonate. However, why is it the case that kinesthetic-vestibular stimulation also facilitates the development of post-hospital discharged prematures and full-term infants of several months chronological age? Within the context of intervention with premature human infants, I find the concept of sensory compensation devoid of explanatory power. A radical extension of compensation might be considered simulation. With regard to approaches that atempt to simulate intrauterine conditions, I entirely agree with Dr. Korner that it "is neither possible nor necessarily desirable." Such attempts have been incomplete and have overlooked the sensory capabilities of the premature neonate, such as vision.

The assumption that hospitalized premature neonates are sensorily deprived and do not share the same sensory experiences as their full-term cohorts has been explicitly stated by several investigators involved in intervention research. In 1976 when Cornell and I published our review paper (Cornell & Gottfried), we noted that infants in modern intensive care units may have available a variety as well as a large amount of stimulation. At that time, there were no systematic data supporting either position. However, a study by Lawson, Daum, and Turkewitz (1977), suggested that prematures suffer not from an inadequate amount of stimulation, but possibly from an inappropriate pattern that may impair the development of sensory integration. It is noteworthy that a method of assessing tactile–visual sensory integration that my colleagues Rose, Bridger, and I have developed discriminates between normal full-term and premature infants (Gottfried, Rose, & Bridger, 1977; Rose, Gottfried, & Bridger, 1978). At 1 year of age, prematures (with age corrections) consistently fail to transfer information about shape across the tactile and visual modalities, whereas full-terms reliably succeed at this task. Getting back to the main point, data do not favor the view that hospitalized prematures are inadequately stimulated. It is difficult to determine whether providing additional kinesthetic-vestibular stimulation to prematures would make their environment more comparable to that of full-term infants, the reason being that the ecological data on the amount, frequency, and quality of kinesthetic-vestibular stimulation for full-terms are lacking. Furthermore, if one wanted to model the sensory stimulation of the intensive care unit to resemble the home environment of full-terms, kinesthetic-vestibular stimulation, in my opinion, would not be the first to be altered. Initially, one might muffle the constant white noise produced by the isolette and change lighting conditions. Normal day–night lighting conditions could be accomplished by simply placing a sunglass or shield above the isolette while still permitting observation of the infant.

In my view, kinesthetic-vestibular stimulation should be emphasized with young infants not because of compensation, simulation, or deprivation, but rather for purely empirical reasons. There is a growing body of evidence with both prematures and full-terms, neonates and older infants, hospital- and home-based programs, and with stimulation administered by machines and by humans showing that kinesthetic-vestibular types of stimulation enhance infant development with no indication of negative side effects. Among the studies I refer to, in addition to Dr. Korner's and Dr. Barnard's, are those by Clark, Kreutzberg, and Chee (1977); Freedman, Boverman, and Freedman (1966); Hasselmeyer (1964); Karwisch (1971); Neal (1968); Porter (1972); Powell (1974); Rice (1977); Siqueland (1969); Solkoff and Matuszak (1975); Solkoff, Yaffe, Weintraub, and Blase (1969); and White and LaBarbara (1976). My emphasis on kinesthetic-vestibular stimulation does not preclude other types of stimulation, such as visual and auditory. I opt for an appropriate and systematic pattern of multimodal stimulation so as to facilitate the development of sensory coordination and integration.

Although the mediating mechanisms and causal relationships between kinesthetic-vestibular stimulation and developmental outcome are unknown, investigators applying this or other forms of stimulation should incorporate the following methodological components into their design to determine why and when stimulation is effective or most effective. First, most investigators have applied stimulation independent of the infants' state. As Korner (1972) pointed out, threshold, type, and magnitude of response to stimulation varies with respect to the infant's state. Thus, administering stimulation in different states may account for differential effectiveness. Second, there is little objective and systematic information in the published intervention programs on infants' concurrent and immediately subsequent reaction to the stimulation. Intervention need not have a direct effect on outcome measures but may be the first link in the casual sequence. I therefore recommend that investigators observe and record how infants react (behaviorally and physiologically) to the types of stimulation applied.

The last issue I deal with in this paper concerns the comparability and generalizability of neonatal period intervention research. In the review article Cornell and I wrote, (Cornell & Gottfried, 1976), a difficult task we were confronted with involved comparing studies so as to put forth generalizations about program effectiveness. It was difficult to account for trends and inconsistent findings because of an inadequate or total lack of descriptions as well as differences among the programs themselves. To achieve greater comparability and external validity three research dimensions require intensive attention: (1) sample characteristics; (2) specification of the nature of intervention and the intensive care unit where intervention is conducted; and (3) outcome or assessment measures.

With respect to sample characteristics, several of the studies we analyzed provided information that was sketchy or neglected to provide information concerning infants' medical status. Sample size and sex distributions were typically given and periodically socioeconomic information was provided; however, lack of detailed and pertinent medical data permeated much of the literature. This persists in some recent published studies. Of the twelve studies reviewed, five gave information on birth weight but not on gestational age and two provided information on gestational age but not on birth weight. Thus, it is not known whether investigators were studying infants small or appropriate for gestational age. Furthermore, it was not uncommon for investigators to describe their samples by selection limits or criteria (e.g., less than 2500 grams or between 28 and 32 weeks gestation), and not give means and standard deviations on subject variables. Both demographic and medical status as well as inclusion and exclusion subject criteria must be made available either in published or unpublished form to investigators in order to establish the effectiveness of different programs. A uniform system of specifying relevant sample characteristics for all studies as suggested by Bell and Hertz (1976) would be highly desirable in this area of research.

Another major factor restricting comparability of findings was the lack of specification as to the amount of intervention. In all studies the duration of each intervention session and frequency of sessions per day were clearly spelled out; however, the number of days of intervention necessary to ascertain the total amount of stimulation was not specified. For example, in one recent study intervention began 72 hours after birth with two 20-minute sessions per day until the infant regained its birth weight and then one 20-minute session per day until the infant was discharged, and in two other studies intervention sessions commenced on the 5th day after birth and continued until infants reached 36 weeks gestational age (see Cornell & Gottfried, 1976). Findings cannot be compared unless we know the exact duration and amount of intervention administered to experimental groups.

A potential source of variation among intervention study findings may prove to be environmental factors within the intensive care unit. The importance of these factors derive from the studies by Katz (1971) and Neal (1968) in which two hospitals were incorporated into each of their methodological designs. The results in both studies showed not only a significant difference between the experimental and control groups, but also a significant difference between hospitals and a significant group-by-hospital interaction. These data provide evidence that situational variables (e.g., nature of stimulation, formulas and feeding schedules, medical and nursing care) should be taken into account. For a detailed description of the physical and social ecology of newborn special-care units, the reader is referred to a recent investigation by Gottfried, Sherman-Brown, Wallace-Lande, King, Coen, and Allen (1980).

Assessing the effects of intervention is a topic that warrants extensive discussion. Due to the time allotted, I put forth only a few points. Virtually all investigators in this area of research have employed multiple assessment measures. The advantage is obvious; the probability of detecting effects of intervention is increased. Depending on age of assessment, investigators have tended to show agreement as to their choice of measure. Moreover, recent studies show a greater reliance on more formal and objective measures than the earlier studies. In the neonatal period, the Neonatal Behavioral Assessment Scale by Brazelton (1973) has been a favorite, and with older infants psychometric sensorimotor scales such as the Bayley Scales of Infant Development have usually been selected. Thus, there appears to be growth in the use of marker variables. However, infant assessment is still in an exploratory stage and investigators should take advantage of recent research developments in this area such as techniques assessing visual and tactile recognition memory and cross-modal functioning. I also suggest that investigators use full-term infants as additional controls in their studies. This procedure is useful when norms are not available for outcome assessment, because it enables the investigator to monitor the effects of intervention on the premature infant, as compared to the development of the full-term. It may also serve as a quasi or indirect comparison among intervention studies.

In conclusion, we are still at the "cutting edge" in this area of research. To date, there have been approximately 20 neonatal period intervention studies and the findings are becoming more interesting and potentially important. We are making some headway in generating findings that lend themselves to comparison; however, we still have a way to go. I hope the present chapter facilitates the process.

ACKNOWLEDGMENTS

Preparation of this chapter was supported by grants from the Thrasher Research Fund, Social and Behavioral Research Program of the National Foundation—March of Dimes (12–15), and the New York State Health Research Council (C106138). Gratitude is extended to Dr. Adele Eskeles Gottfried for her critical reading of the manuscript and to Dr. Vincent L. Smeriglio for his invitation to participate.

REFERENCES

Bell, R. Q., & Hertz, T. W. Toward more comparability and generalizability of developmental research. *Child Development,* 1976, *47,* 6–13.

Brazelton, T. B. Neonatal behavioral assessment scale. *Clinics in Developmental Medicine* (No. 50). Philadelphia: J. P. Lippincott, 1973.

Clark, D. L., Kreutzberg, J. R., & Chee, F. K. W. Vestibular stimulation influence on motor development in infants. *Science,* 1977, *196,* 1228–1229.

Cornell, E. H., & Gottfried, A. W. Intervention with premature human infants. *Child Development,* 1976, *47,* 32–39.

Freedman, D. G., Boverman, H., & Freedman, N. *Effects of kinesthetic stimulation on weight gain and on smiling in premature infants.* Paper presented at the annual meeting of the American Orthopsychiatric Association, San Francisco, April 1966.

Gottfried, A. W., Rose, S. A., & Bridger, W. H. Cross-modal transfer in human infants. *Child Development,* 1977, *48,* 118–123.

Gottfried, A. W., Sherman-Brown, S., Wallace-Lande, P., King, J. C., Coen, C., & Allen, M. K. *Physical and social ecology of newborn special-care units.* Paper presented at International Conference on Infant Studies, New Haven, April 1980.

Hasselmeyer, E. G. The premature's response to handling. *American Nurses Association*, 1964, *11*, 15–24.

Karwisch, G. A. The effects of early experiences on conditioned head turning in the human newborn. (Unpublished doctoral dissertation, Purdue University, 1971). *Dissertation Abstracts International*, 1971, *32*, 3639–B. (University Microfilms No. 72–18974)

Katz, V. Auditory stimulation and developmental behavior of the premature infant. *Nursing Research*, 1971, *20*, 196–201.

Korner, A. F. State as variable, as obstacle, and as mediator of stimulation in infant research. *Merrill-Palmer Quarterly*, 1972, *18*, 77–94.

Lawson, K., Daum, C., & Turkewitz, G. Environmental characteristics of a neonatal intensive-care unit. *Child Development*, 1977, *48*, 1633–1639.

Neal, M. V. Vestibular stimulation and developmental behavior of the small premature infant. *Nursing Research Reports*, 1968, *3*, 2–5.

Porter, L. S. The impact of physical-physiological activity on infants' growth and development. *Nursing Research*, 1972, *21*, 210–219.

Powell, L. F. The effect of extra stimulation and maternal involvement on the development of low-birth-weight infants and on maternal behavior. *Child Development*, 1974, *45*, 106–113.

Rice, R. D. Neurophysiological development in premature infants following stimulation. *Developmental Psychology*, 1977, *13*, 69–76.

Rose, S. A., Gottfried, A. W., & Bridger, W. H. Cross-modal transfer in infants: Relationship to prematurity and socioeconomic background. *Developmental Psychology*, 1978, *14*, 643–652.

Scarr-Salapatek, S., & Williams, M. L. A stimulation program for low-birth-weight infants. *American Journal of Public Health*, 1972, *62*, 662–667.

Scarr-Salapatek, S., & Williams, M. L. The effects of early stimulation on low-birth-weight infants. *Child Development*, 1973, *44*, 94–101.

Siqueland, E. R. *Further developments in infant learning*. Paper presented at the 19th International Congress of Psychology, London, 1969.

Solkoff, N., & Matuszak, D. Tactile stimulation and behavioral development among low-birthweight infants. *Child Psychiatry and Human Development*, 1975, *6*, 33–37.

Solkoff, N., Yaffe, S., Weintraub, D., & Blase, B. Effects of handling on the subsequent development of premature infants. *Developmental Psychology*, 1969, *1*, 765–768.

White, J. L., & LaBarbara, R. C. The effects of tactile and kinesthetic stimulation on neonatal development in the premature infant. *Developmental Psychobiology*, 1976, *9*, 569–577.

PARENT–INFANT CONTACT

7 Extra Postpartum Contact: An Assessment of the Intervention and Its Effects

Mary Anne Trause
The Fairfax Hospital
and
Georgetown University School of Medicine

Over the last 8 years a number of studies have been done to examine the effects of extra postpartum contact between mothers and their full-term newborns on maternal attachment and behavior. Robson and Moss (1970) have defined maternal attachment in a way that is useful for this discussion. They describe maternal attachment as the extent to which a mother feels that her infant occupies an essential position in her life. Its components include:

1. Feelings of warmth or love.
2. A sense of possession, devotion, protectiveness, and concern for the infant's well-being.
3. A positive anticipation of prolonged contact.
4. An acceptance of impositions and obligations intolerable from less important objects.
5. A sense of loss experienced with the infant's actual or imagined absence.

INTERVENTION

In all but one of the studies of extra contact, comparisons have been made of the behavior of two groups of mothers: one group experiencing the amount of postpartum contact dictated by contemporary hospital routine, the other experiencing additional contact in the first hours and days of life. The first study conducted by Drs. Kennell and Klaus offers a good example of this type of intervention. The control group of mothers who received the care that was routine in the hospital at that time saw their babies momentarily after birth before they were taken to the nursery, and saw them again briefly at 6–8 hours for identification, followed by

20–30 minute visits every 4 hours for feeding. In contrast, the experimental mothers were given their naked babies in bed with them for 1 hour within the first 3 hours after birth and for 5 extra hours on each of the next 3 days of life. Thus, the intervention consisted of 16 extra hours of contact during the hospital stay (Kennell, Jerauld, Wolfe, Chesler, Kreger, McAlpine, Steffa, & Klaus, 1974; Klaus, Jerauld, Kreger, McAlpine, Steffa, & Kennell, 1972).

The rationale for this intervention was based on the following premises:

1. The newborn infant's immediate survival and long-term development are dependent on his or her receiving care from an adult who is emotionally attached to him or her.

2. Studies of infra-human mammals and clinical experience with mothers of premature and sick infants suggest that separation of a mother from her young in the immediate postpartum period interferes with the developmentof this maternal behavior and attachment.

3. Considering the cultural expectations of the mother of a full-term infant and the physiological changes she has undergone, it seems reasonable to hypothesize that the immediate postpartum period is a time of maximum sensitivity for her, too. Therefore, the separation of healthy mothers and newborns dictated by hospital routines is also likely to affect the development of maternal behavior and attachment, especially in groups of mothers subject to other sources of stress.

Since Klaus and Kennell's original study, a number of others with similar designs have been conducted. Although all have compared the effects of routine and extra contact experiences, the extra contact interventions have varied on the following dimensions:

1. The length of time after birth when initial contact began, e.g., immediately (deChateau, 1976), or second day (O'Connor, Vietze, Hopkins, & Altemeier, 1977).

2. The length of time the contact lasted, e.g., 15 minutes (deChateau, 1976), or 16 hours (Kennell et al., 1974; Klaus et al., 1972).

3. The number of visits constituting the extra contact, e.g., one (deChateau, 1976), or four (Kennell et al., 1974; Klaus et al., 1972).

4. The type of interaction structured into the contact, e.g., breastfeeding (Johnson, 1976), or skin-to-skin contact (Sosa, Klaus, Kennell, & Urrutia, 1976).

5. Where the contact occurred, e.g., the delivery room (deChateau, 1976), or mother's room (O'Connor et al., 1977).

6. Who was present, e.g., the father (deChateau, 1976), or a breastfeeding specialist (Sousa, Burros, Gazalle, Begeres, Pinheiro, Monezes, & Arruda, 1974).

Basically, the studies have tested the effects of the intervention as a whole rather than attempting to tease out the contributions of particular variables. The only exceptions to this were carried out by Hales and her colleagues (Hales, Lozoff, Sosa, & Kennell, 1977) who, using three groups, varied the time when the intervention began, and by Kontos (1978) who, using four groups, tested the separate effects of two factors; contact in the 1st hour after birth, and rooming-in beginning at 24 hours.

SAMPLES

Although the characteristics of the samples have varied between studies, they have been relatively homogeneous within single studies. Klaus and Kennell's original sample included low-income, young, black American urban women, who were primarily single. Since then, studies have included middle-class, married, Swedish (deChateau, 1976) and Canadian (Kontos, 1978) women; low-income urban, primarily single Guatemalan women (Sosa et al., 1976); low-income Brazilian women (Sousa et al., 1974); and middle-income American women (Johnson, 1976). Most of the studies have included only primiparous mothers with the exception of deChateau (1976), who included and compared the behavior of multips and primips.

MEASURES

The measures used in these studies are somewhat uniform as a result of the fact that several of the studies have come from the same research group and some collaboration has already occurred among groups. The research done by Klaus and Kennell and their colleagues falls into two categories: studies of maternal attachment behavior and those interested in breastfeeding. In the original study by Klaus and Kennell (Kennell et al., 1974; Klaus et al., 1972), three measures proved useful in determining the effects of extra postpartum contact on maternal attachment. These included filmed observations of mothers feeding their babies 1 month after hospital discharge, observations of mothers' behavior during a physical examination of their babies at 1 month and 1 year, and mothers' answers to questions included in a 1-month and 1-year medical history of their babies. Collaboration with Dr. Ringler, a psycholinguist, yielded a number of additional measures of the mothers' speech to their children when they were 1 and 2 years old, and of the children's IQs and speech and language comprehension when 5 years old (Ringler, Kennell, Jarvella, Navojosky, & Klaus, 1975; Ringler, Trause, Klaus, & Kennell, 1978).

The first of these measures, mothers' behavior during feeding has been used in modified form in three studies besides the original one. Feeding was chosen as a measure of maternal attachment because of its universality and its central position in the mother–infant relationship—especially with young infants. In addition, it can be carried out as a purely perfunctory caregiving task or as an affectionate interplay between mother and infant. Thus, the frequency of a number of caregiving behaviors, such as position of the bottle, burping and face-wiping, were calculated from the 10-minute time-lapse films as well as affectionate or attachment behaviors, such as fondling and looking en face. The film was taken at one frame per second, which yielded 600 frames for the 10-minute period analyzed. These films were made at discharge and 1 month later.

This measure was later modified by Hales et al. (1977) and deChateau (1976), who moved to a live, 15-minute time sample observation of feeding within the infant's first 2 days of life. Many of the same behaviors were observed although Hales grouped them on a theoretical basis into three scores rather than looking at them primarily as individual measures. The first variable reflected affectionate behavior, which included looking at the baby, looking en face, talking to the baby, and fondling, kissing, and smiling at the baby. The second variable, proximity-maintaining behavior, consisted of holding the infant, holding the infant close or encompassing the infant, and the location of the infant (i.e., mother's bed or chair, own bed near mother, or own bed far from mother). A total caretaking score was determined from the sum of the frequencies of diapering, burping, and covering. In Hales' first study she observed mothers and infants at 12 hours, whereas in her second study and that of deChateau, observations were made at 36 hours. In addition, deChateau used many of the same measures of maternal affectionate behavior during his observations of play in the home at 3 months, as did Kontos (1978) at both 1 and 3 months.

The second measure used by Klaus and Kennell, the observation of maternal behavior during a stressful physical examination, was designed to tap the mothers' sense of protectiveness and concern for the infants' well-being. During 10-minute physical examinations carried out when infants were 1 month and 1 year old, the mothers' behavior was observed through a one-way mirror and recorded every 15 seconds. Variables included where she was located with respect to the physician and infant (e.g., at the tableside or across the room), whether she was watching or assisting the physician, and how she responded to her infant's cries. This measure has not been reported by other investigators.

The third measure consisted of a number of questions included in the medical history designed to elicit the mother's ability to respond to the infant's needs and to indicate whether she experienced a sense of loss with the infant's absence. Examples of questions included "When the baby cries, has been fed, and diapers are dry, what do you do?" and "Have you gone out since the infant was born? How did you feel?" Other investigators have not reported the use of this measure either.

Ringler and her colleagues (Ringler et al., 1975; 1978) added the examination of maternal linguistic behavior and children's speech and language comprehension to the measures used to study the effects of extra postpartum contact within this sample. During a free-play period, all dialogue between mother and child was tape-recorded and simultaneously transcribed by observers viewing them through a one-way mirror. The 10-minute sequence of utterances was classified according to the following standard linguistic criteria: the number of adjectives, the number of words per proposition, the mean utterance length, the proportion of content words, and the proportion of statements, commands, and questions. These data were collected when children were 1 and 2 years of age. When the children were 5, they were administered three standardized tests of intellectual and linguistic functioning—the Stanford–Binet (Form L–M), the Assessment of Children's Language Comprehension (Foster, Giddan, & Stark, 1973), and The Northwest Syntax (Lee, 1969). The Assessment of Children's Language Comprehension (ACLC) is a four-part test including Part A, which assesses vocabulary comprehension, and Parts B, C, and D, which evaluate children's comprehension of phrases with an increasing number of critical elements. For example, Part B includes phrases such as "horse standing," which contains two critical elements in contrast to the phrases in Part D, such as "happy little girl running," which contains four. The Northwest Syntax is a two-part test assessing children's expressive ability and their receptive comprehension of grammar.

Measures used by Klaus, Kennell, and Ringler, which did not identify differences between the groups included the Bayley, Stanford–Binet, and language tests, a rating scale of the mother's perception of herself and of the baby in the newborn period, and observations of behavior during the free-play and Bayley testing sessions at 1 year.

A second group of studies carried out by Kennell and Klaus and their colleagues was designed to determine the effects of extra postpartum contact on variables related to breastfeeding (Sosa et al., 1976). The underlying assumption was that incrased contact in the early postpartum period would influence the development of maternal attachment, which in turn would affect the success of breastfeeding. In underdeveloped countries where the termination of breastfeeding is associated with increased rates of infant morbidity and mortality, longer breastfeeding should be associated with improved infant health and development. Thus, these studies examined the effects of extra postpartum contact on the length of breastfeeding, infant weight gain and the incidence of infection. Data were collected several times during the 1st year of life.

Three other studies (deChateau, 1976; Johnson, 1976; Sousa et al., 1974) have also compared the percentage of women breastfeeding after 2 or 3 months following routine contact or extra contact, which included nursing in the 1st hour after birth. However, these investigators did not identify attachment as an explanatory construct.

One group of investigators (O'Connor et al., 1977) used unique measures to test the effects of extra postpartum contact. O'Connor and her colleagues studied the incidence of parenting disturbances or failure resulting in infant hospitalization within the first 21 months of life.

FINDINGS

Despite the variations in the parameters of the extra-contact intervention between studies, the findings have been relatively consistent. In fact, in every study except one, the extra-contact group surpassed the controls on at least some measures, whereas in only one did the controls significantly surpass the experimentals at all. Considering the group of studies as a whole, extra contact between mother and newborn has affected maternal affectionate behavior during feeding, protectiveness during a physical examination, attitude toward leaving the child, pattern of speaking to the child, affectionate behavior during play, length of breastfeeding, and incidence of parenting disorder. It has also been related to infant weight gain and expressiveness during play. The measures that have shown effects of the intervention most consistently are maternal affectionate behavior, especially en face in the first 3 months, and the length of breastfeeding. Measures of performance on standardized developmental, language, and intelligence tests have been the least useful in identifying differences between the groups, although the language comprehension scores did indicate different patterns of relationship between maternal speech and children's speech and language comprehension in each group (Ringler et al., 1978).

RESEARCH PROGRESS

These findings clearly underline that contact during the early postpartum period does influence subsequent maternal and infant behavior. Further research in this area is important both for our theoretical understanding of maternal attachment and the onset of extrauterine mother–infant interaction and for the establishment of policies and alternative institutions to provide optimum perinatal care. For our knowledge to grow, researchers must tackle three types of studies. Some of these would benefit from collaboration among investigators; others would be likely to advance most quickly if undertaken by individuals or independent research groups.

The first priority should be to determine, if possible, which parameters of the intervention of putting mothers and infants together soon after birth are associated with the changes in behavior. Is the time after birth when the intervention begins important?Does the father's presence or the type of interaction that occurs affect the outcome? To answer these and related questions that are especially important for establishing hospital policy, investigators must systematically vary one or two factors within each design. Collaboration among independent investigators using the same outcome measures would be most fruitful in this area. Then results could be combined to tease out the important components of the intervention. However, given the rich findings from the existing studies that contain a wide variation in these parameters, it is conceivable that the contact with the newborn, regardless of how it is structured, is what influences the mother. Thus, I would argue that new studies varying one or two factors should also include control groups without extra contact. For example, a study testing the effects of father presence should have at least three groups: extra contact with fathers present, extra contact without fathers present, and controls without extra contact. Then if there is no difference between the two contact groups (i.e., with and without fathers present), we can still determine if the contact with the infant influences maternal behavior. The neatest design to answer the question of the influence of father presence would be a 2 × 2 factorial design with the two factors being: (1) infant presence; and (2) father presence during the specified time soon after birth. Thus, one group of mothers would have only infants present, one would have only fathers, one would have both, and one would have neither.

In addition to the systematic testing of intervention parameters, these studies should, where feasible, include heterogeneous samples, which vary in at least one characteristic, e.g., parity, income, or childbirth preparation. We could then determine how aspects of the intervention affect particular groups of women. For example, perhaps having father present is important for primips, but not for multips. These kinds of data would be invaluable for practitioners attempting to fit care patterns to individual needs.

A second important line of research might be most productive if carried out by independent scientists or groups. The research to date has demonstrated that extra postpartum contact affects certain aspects of maternal and infant behavior, but it has not indicated how. The antecedent–consequence format of the studies to date has not examined the process through which extra contact with the newborn in the early postpartum period affects behavior. To determine the mechanisms, we need different measures than those already used in order to focus on and follow the mother–infant interaction as it develops longitudinally. Perhaps a device such as Sander's (Sander, Stechler, Burns, & Julia, 1970) stabilimeter, which yields continuous data on infant activity and caregiver intervention, would be a valuable means of examining the question of process. Likewise, Stern's (1974) procedures for studying dyadic gazing might reveal different patterns of interaction between mothers and infants with and without extra postpartum contact. In the best of all possible worlds, independent researchers using unique outcome measures might coordinate the parameters of their interventions and sample characteristics in order to increase the comparability of their studies. It would also be useful for these investigators to include some "marker variables" (Bell & Hertz, 1976), such as maternal en face behavior or length of breastfeeding to anchor their new efforts to the already existing body of research.

Last, but not least, we need more basic research on maternal attachment. I think the assumption that effecting enduring changes in infant behavior and development is best accomplished through effecting changes in the mother is a reasonable one. Yet, we need to document the relationship between maternal behaviors affected by extra contact, such as the amount of en face, and infant development. Bruner (1976) has observed that for mothers and older infants, looking en face plays a special role in the development of preverbal communication. He suggests that mothers and their 6- or 7-month-olds look en face in the process of pointing to an object to check whether their gesturing is "getting through" to the other. To complement this, we found, in a post analysis of the data from Klaus and Kennell's original study, that the amount mothers looked en face at their infants during feeding at 1 month was significantly correlated with the amount mothers talked to their infants during free play at 1 year. We can speculate that looking en face at a 1-month-old is an attempt to monitor and read the infant's expression in the same way that looking en face at a 6- or 7-month old is an attempt to read his or her understanding of a gesture. Perhaps this function of looking en face is accomplished by talking to a 1-year-old. But what is the effect of mothers looking en face on infant behavior? We do not have the data to even speculate on the answer to that question.

Likewise, we do not yet have the data to confirm that looking en face is indeed a measure of maternal attachment. A central component of the notion of attachment is that one is attached to specific individuals, not people in general. Yet, we do not know whether mothers look en face at their own babies to whom they are presumably attached more than they look en face at babies in general. In other words, which maternal behaviors are valid indicators of attachment and which are merely the social responses any baby is likely to elicit? This is a new enough area of research that the efforts of independent researchers would probably be most productive at first.

In conclusion, Dr. Kennell and Dr. Klaus have identified an extremely fruitful and important area of research in their studies of the effects of extra postpartum contact on maternal behavior and attachment. Now other researchers with individual areas of expertise can apply their knowledge and methods to the challenging questions that remain: (1) which particular factors are associated with the beneficial effects of the extra contact experience; (2) how does the experience affect subsequent attachment; and, (3) what is maternal attachment? Understanding maternal attachment and its determinants is tremendously important both for our theories of human development and for our hospital practices in the perinatal period.

REFERENCES

Bell, R. Q., & Hertz, T. W. Toward more comparability and generalizability of developmental research. *Child Development,* 1976, *47,* 6–13.

Bruner, J. S. From communication to language—a psychological perspective. *Cognition,* 1976, *3,* 255–287.

deChateau, P. The influence of early contact on maternal and infant behavior in primiparae. *Birth and the Family Journal,* 1976, *3,* 149–155.

Foster, R., Giddan, J. J., & Stark, J. *Assessment of children's language comprehension*. Palo Alto, Calif.: Consulting Psychologists Press, 1973.

Hales, D. J., Lozoff, B., Sosa, R., & Kennell, J. H. Defining the limits of the maternal sensitive period. *Developmental Medicine and Child Neurology*, 1977, *19*, 454–461.

Johnson, N. W. Breastfeeding at one hour of age. *American Journal of Maternal and Child Nursing*, 1976, *1*, 12.

Kennell, J. H., Jerauld, R., Wolfe, H., Chesler, D., Kreger, N. C., McAlpine, W., Steffa, M., & Klaus, M. H. Maternal behavior one year after early and extended post-partum contact. *Developmental Medicine and Child Neurology*, 1974, *16*, 172–179.

Klaus, M. H., Jerauld, R., Kreger, N., McAlpine, W., Steffa, M., & Kennell, J. H. Maternal attachment: Importance of the first post-partum days, *New England Journal of Medicine*, 1972, *286*, 460–463.

Kontos, D. A study of the effects of extended mother–infant contact on maternal behavior at one and three months. *Birth and the Family Journal*, 1978, *5*, 133–140.

Lee, L. *Northwest Syntax Screening Test*. Evanston, Ill.: Northwestern University Press, 1969.

O'Connor, S. M., Vietze, P. M., Hopkins, J. B., & Altemeier, W. A. Postpartum extended maternal–infant contact: Subsequent mothering and child health. *Society for Pediatric Research*, 1977, *11*, 380. (Abstract)

Ringler, N. M., Kennell, J. H., Jarvella, R., Navojosky, B. J., & Klaus, M. H. Mother-to-child speech at two years—effects of early postnatal contact. *Journal of Pediatrics*, 1975, *86*, 141–144.

Ringler, N. M., Trause, M. A., Klaus, M. H., & Kennell, J. H. The effects of extra post-partum contact and maternal speech patterns on children's IQs, speech, and language comprehension at 5. *Child Development*, 1978, *49*, 862–865.

Robson, K. S., & Moss, H. A. Patterns and determinants of maternal attachment. *Journal of Pediatrics*, 1970, *77*, 976–985.

Sander, L. W., Stechler, G., Burns, P., & Julia, J. Early mother–infant interaction and 24-hour patterns of activity and sleep. *Journal of the American Academy of Child Psychiatry*, 1970, *9*, 103–123.

Sosa, R., Klaus, M. H., Kennell, J. H., & Urrutia, J. J. The effect of early mother–infant contact on breastfeeding, infection, and growth. In *Breastfeeding and the Infant* (Ciba Foundation Symposium 45). Amsterdam: Elsevier Publishing Company, 1976.

Sousa, P. L. R., Burros, F. C., Gazalle, R. V., Begeres, R. M., Pinheiro, G. N., Monezes, S. T., & Arruda, L. A. *Attachment and lactation*. XIV Congreso Internacional de Pediatria, Buenos Aires, Argentina, 1974.

Stern, D. Mother and infant at play: The dyadic interaction involving facial, vocal, and gaze behaviors. In M. Lewis & L. A. Rosenblum (Eds.), *The effect of the infant on its caregiver*. New York: John Wiley, 1974.

8 Mother–Infant Separation: Outcome Assessment

Marjorie J. Seashore
San Francisco State University

An intensive study of the effect of prolonged separation of mothers and their infants was conducted by a research group headed by P. Herbert Leiderman and Clifford R. Barnett at the Stanford University School of Medicine. The significant substantive findings from this study have previously been reported in several articles (Barnett, Leiderman, Grobstein, & Klaus, 1970; Leiderman, 1978; Leiderman, Leifer, Seashore, Barnett, & Grobstein, 1973; Leiderman & Seashore, 1975; Leifer, Leiderman, Barnett, & Williams, 1972; Seashore, Leifer, Barnett, & Leiderman, 1973).

Given the current concern with issues of comparability and generalizability of findings from this and other studies, this paper is devoted to reporting the many outcome measures used in this study, as well as summarizing the findings with respect to each measure, whether or not such measures demonstrated significant effects or were determined to be adequate operationalizations of the key variables in the final analysis. By concentrating on the methodological aspects of the study, we can then identify some of the key problems in making assessments and comparisons across studies.

As indicated, the focus of this research on mothers and infants was on the effect of prolonged separation of a mother from her infant during the neonatal period. The central question is the effects of such separation on maternal attitudes and behavior toward the infant, and on the infant's subsequent development.

The group's interest in this area developed from clinical observations of the attitudes and behavior of mothers toward their premature infants with whom they had only visual contact during the 3 to 12 weeks the infant was hospitalized after birth. Mothers reported feelings of detachment toward these infants and, when finally allowed to hold and care for their infants in the discharge nursery, appeared ill at ease and unresponsive to the infant. Literature on the effects of long-term separation on infant development (Ainsworth, 1962; Bowlby, Ainsworth, Boston, & Rosenbluth, 1956; Spitz, 1954) and on the effects of separation on maternal behavior of animals toward their young (Klopfer, Adams, & Klopfer, 1964; Moore, 1968; Noirot, 1964; Rosenblatt & Lehrman, 1963) suggested that the separation experience might have long-lasting detrimental effects on the development of the mother–infant relationship and on infant development.

The mother separated from her premature infant is deprived of all stimulus contact beyond limited visual contact. Even with visual contact, the mother is severely limited in the extent to which she can observe the responsiveness of her infant either in general, or more critically, to her presence or actions. The establishment of eye-to-eye contact, which Robson (1967) has suggested is important for the development of infant–mother attachment, is all but impossible. Furthermore, the mother is prevented from fulfilling her expected role as mother. It is a nurse, not she, who is caring for her infant's physical and emotional needs—feeding, soothing, and showing affection to the infant.

This deprivation experience occurs during a time when mothers are likely to be most psychologically primed to assume the maternal role. From the research of Bibring, Dwyer, Huntington, and Valenstein (1961), it is known that maternal feelings in primigravidae are markedly enhanced in the presence of movement of the fetus at 5 months. These maternal expectancies continue to increase only to be abruptly interrupted by the premature birth. This may be at a time when the mother has not yet fully prepared herself for enactment of her new role. The absence of contact with the infant may result in promoting a sense of remoteness from the infant she has seen only briefly. With the premature infant, this sense of remoteness may be heightened by uncertainty as to the child's health or viability. Without physical contact with the child there is little opportunity for reassurance that the child is a real and responding human being. Nor is there opportunity for establishing a close, reciprocal relationship with the child.

The clinical observations and literature on separation led to the development of a sequence of hypotheses about the effects of separation on mother and infant. The first hypothesis was that, for the mother, separation would lead to decreased ability to cope with stress, a lowered sense of commitment (or attachment) to the infant, and a lowered level of self-confidence in her ability to care for the needs of her infant. These attitudes were expected to influence, and be expressed in, lower levels of attachment behavior toward the infant, less stimulation of the infant and less skillful behavior in caring for the infant once contact had been resumed. It was further hypothesized that these attitudes and behaviors might adversely affect the physical and psychological development of the infant over time. Although primarily interested in this causal sequence, we also recognized that once contact had been established, the infant's state and behavior would also influence maternal attitudes and behavior.

SAMPLE

The study design consisted of a comparison of two groups of mothers and premature infants: a Separation group in which the mother (and infant) experienced the then usual physical separation of 3 to 12 weeks until shortly before the infant was ready to go home, and a Contact group in which mothers were permitted into the intensive care nursery to handle and care for their infants as often as they wished during the entire hospitalization period. A third group of mothers and their normal, full-term infants was also studied to provide a basis of comparison for the mothers of premature infants. The final sample consisted of 24 mothers and infants in the Separation group, 22 in the Contact group, and 24 in the Full-Term Comparison group. The study of each mother–infant pair extended from birth to 21 months after the infant's discharge from the hospital.

The study was limited to those mothers and infants who met the following criteria:

1. The mother had no previous history of premature or low-birthweight infants.
2. The infant was free from obvious congenital abnormalities.
3. The infant was not a multiple birth.
4. If premature, the infant weighed from 890 to 1899 grams (2.0 to 4.2 pounds) at birth.
5. There was a father present in the home.

Conditions in the nursery alternated between Separation and Contact at predetermined intervals of from 3 to 6 months duration. The assignment of mother and infant to the Separation or Contact group was thus determined by which condition interval the nursery was in at the time of birth. Mothers of full-term infants were selected so as to be comparable to those in the premature groups in terms of parity, sex of infant, and social class. All three groups were predominantly middle class and white, although not exclusively so. The median age for mothers was 24–25 and the median educational level for both mothers and fathers was some college short of a B.A. degree. Each group included both primiparous and multiparous mothers, and male and female infants, although their numbers were not equally distributed among groups. Because of differences in distribution, all analyses of the data took parity and sex into account. It is important to note that, due to the locale of the study, the study population was not typical of families with premature infants—being older, from a higher socioeconomic background, white, and having both parents present in the home.

MEASURES

Intervention consisted of allowing mothers in the Contact group to enter the nursery to handle and care for their infants throughout hospitalization. Mothers in the Separation group were allowed into the nursery only after the infant had entered the discharge nursery, approximately 1 week prior to discharge. At a given time all mothers with infants in the nursery were either Separation or Contact. Neither group of mothers realized that the nursery procedures varied over time and therefore between groups.

Following from our hypotheses, the outcome measures used fall into three general categories—maternal attitudes, maternal behavior, and infant development. Each is in turn further divided into subcategories.

Maternal Attitudes

Mothers' attitudes in each of three areas—coping, commitment, and self-confidence—were determined through a combination of interviews and questionnaires. Interviews were all transcribed and subsequently coded both for specific responses elicited by each question and on the three attitudinal dimensions. Mothers were interviewed four to six times while the infant was hospitalized, and at 1, 6, 12, and 21 months after the infant had been discharged from the hospital. We thus could make comparisons among groups at particular points in time and assess changes in a mother's attitudes over time.

The responses to questionnaires were analyzed using both summary measures and individual items. These questionnaires provided information on coping, commitment, and self-confidence each time the mother was interviewed.

Coping. Two questionnaires related to the mother's adaptation to stress or how well she was coping emotionally with her current situation. The Cornell Medical Index was used to have some measure of psychological distress being experienced by the mothers. This was administered after the first visit to the discharge nursery and after the infant had been home for 6 months. The Nowlis Mood Adjective Checklist was filled out at each interview. This questionnaire contains 40 adjectives for which the mother indicates how well, if at all, each describes her mood during the past 24 hours.

Commitment. A mother's feelings of commitment to her infant were measured by a comparison of her description of her own infant with her description of what she considered an "ideal" infant using a semantic differential questionnaire. Ten adjective pairs were presented: sturdy–fragile, irritable–calm, healthy–sick, alert–drowsy, sad–happy, careful–impulsive, plain–pretty, active–passive, light–heavy, and stiff–cuddly. In analyzing the questionnaires, both the actual responses to her own infant and the discrepancies between responses for her infant and her "ideal" infant were compared.

The *Maternal Attitude Scale* developed by Dr. Bert Cohler was used as a measure of the mother's general commitment to the maternal role and attitudes toward children and childrearing. This questionnaire consists of over 200 items that have been factor analyzed into a number of summary scores such as the mother's attitude toward the independence of her child. Mothers filled out this questionnaire near the time the infant was discharged and again 12 months later.

We also attempted to record the frequency of a mother's visits to the hospital while the infant was hospitalized and the frequency of phone calls to the nursery, but these data are incomplete.

Self-confidence. A paired-comparison questionnaire was used to assess a mother's confidence in her ability to care for her infant. Mothers were presented with successive pairs of possible caretakers for the infant and asked to choose which, within each pair, she thought could best care for her baby. The choices of caretakers were herself, an "experienced" mother, the infant's father, the infant's grandmother, a pediatric nurse, and a doctor. Mothers made these choices for each of six caretaking tasks. For purposes of anlaysis, these tasks were classified as either social or instrumental. Tasks defined as social were calming the baby, understanding what the baby wants, and showing affection to the baby. Instrumental tasks were feeding, diapering, and bathing the baby. While the infant was in the hospital, the mother was asked to respond in terms of her choices if the baby were being cared for under normal circumstances. Responses were analyzed both by using a standard paired-comparison scoring technique and by simply computing the percentage of times when, given the choice of herself or another caretaker, a mother chose herself.

Maternal Behaviors

Mothers were observed caring for their infants in the discharge nursery (or, for the mothers of full-term infants, on the maternity ward), at home 1 week after discharge, in the pediatrics clinic at 1 and 6 months after discharge, and again at home at 11 and 21 months after discharge. Each observation was scheduled to occur while the mother was engaging in specified routine caretaking tasks such as feeding, diapering, and bathing the infant. The 11- and 21-month observations also included a specified period of time during which the mother was not engaged in caretaking tasks. The observation period extended throughout the time the mother was performing the specified activities. Observations were made at 15-second intervals using a checklist of frequently occurring maternal and infant behaviors as well as writing down other, less frequently occurring behaviors. Because of the varying lengths of time of the observations, behaviors were measured as percentages of time mother and/or infant were engaged in a particular activity or behavior. Our particular interest in these observations was in behaviors relating to skill and attachment.

Skill. A summary skill score was derived for the early observations that included: (1) the percentage of total intervals that the infant was not crying; (2) the percentage of feeding intervals during which the infant was not sucking that the mother stimulated the infant to suck; (3) the percentage of feeding intervals during which the bottle was in the infant's mouth that the infant was sucking; (4) the percentage of intervals during which the mother was feeding the infant that she did not remove the bottle without burping the infant.

Attachment. Two categories of attachment behaviors were analyzed. Distal attachment behaviors included looking, talking, laughing, and smiling at the infant. Holding, affectionate tuching, and ventral contact during holding were categorized as proximal attachment behaviors. These behaviors were generally analyzed individually rather than summed within categories because of the low and inconsistent correlations among behaviors within a given category.

Infant Development

The infant's mental and motor development were measured using the Bayley Scales of Infant Development. Each infant was tested in the discharge nursery, and subsequently at 3, 9, 15, and 21 months after discharge. Only the raw scores were used because of the difficulty in applying norms based on the development of full-term infants to the premature infants in our study. Pediatric assessments of the infant's health, height, and weight were made during hospitalization and at 1, 6, 12, and 21 months after discharge.

Other Variables

In order to control for differences among mothers and infants that might influence outcome, we collected extensive information on family background and the infant's status while hospitalized. The principal demographic variables used in the analyses were social class as determined by the father's occupation using both the Warner Index of Social Class (Warner, Meeker, & Ells, 1949) and the Hollingshead Index (which also takes education into account), mother's educational level, and mother's social class background as measured by her father's occupation. Parity of the mother was also considered.

Infant variables included sex, birthweight, Apgar score, health–sickness ratings made during hospitalization, and measures of the activity level and sleeping-waking-crying behavior during each of two 24-hour periods in the hospital.

SUMMARY OF FINDINGS

In general, we found relatively few differences between those mothers and infants who had been kept separated and those who had been in contact during hospitalization. Our interpretations of some of the reasons for this are given later following a summary of our major findings. Except when otherwise noted, levels of statistical significance were based on two-way analyses of variance measuring effects of Separation–Contact and parity or sex.

Maternal Attitudes

Coping and Commitment.   There were no differences between groups in coping or in expressed commitment to the infant. In making this statement, we rely very heavily on the information gathered from interviews. In retrospect we have some rather serious reservations about the questionnaire measures we used. Unlike the self-confidence questionnaire, each involved some perhaps questionable assumptions in interpretation, as well as other methodological problems.

Self-confidence.   We did find that the denial of mother–infant interaction experienced by the Separation group had a negative effect on maternal self-confidence for primiparous mothers and for those who were initially low in self-confidence. Primiparous mothers in the Separation group were less confident than primiparous mothers in the Contact group regarding both social and instrumental caretaking tasks while the infant was in the discharge nursery ($p < .01$), although there had been no significant difference between them earlier. At 1 month after discharge, mothers in the Separation group were still less confident regarding instrumental tasks ($p < .05$), but there was no difference in confidence regarding social tasks. Looking only at mothers who were initially low in confidence within each group, by the time the infant was in the discharge nursery mothers in the contact group had increased significantly in confidence compared to those in the Separation group for both social tasks ($p < .02$) and instrumental tasks ($p < .01$), as indicated by Chi-square analysis. These differences coincide with those obtained from ratings of interviews with these mothers.

The mother's level of self-confidence on instrumental tasks at the time of the infant's discharge from the hospital was significantly related to her observed skill at the 1 week home observation ($p < .05$) using multiple regression analysis controlling for parity, sex of infant, and exact number of days since discharge that the observation was made. This, however, was the only relationship found between self-confidence and observed skill behavior. Maternal self-confidence was also positively related to infant development in the first months. Maternal self-confidence predicted increases in mental and motor scores of premature infants from discharge to 3 months after discharge ($p < .01$), using multiple regression analyses controlling for sex, birthweight, and the infant's mental or motor score at discharge as well as the mother's parity, treatment group, observed level of attachment behavior, and expressed level of commitment to the infant at 1 month.

Maternal Behaviors

Skill. Mothers in the Separation group were slightly less skillful at the first observation in the discharge nursery than were mothers in the Contact group ($p < .10$), but not subsequently. This difference was greater for mothers of females in each group than for mothers of males, with the difference between mothers of females in the Separation and Contact groups significant at the .05 level. Within the Contact group, mothers of females were more skillful when observed in the discharge nursery than were mothers of males ($p < .05$), consistent with the findings of Moss (1967) on two measures—crying and stimulating to feed—included in the skill summary score we used.

Attachment. We found no differences between Separation and Contact mothers in either distal or proximal attachment behaviors. Mothers of full-term infants, however, showed more affectionate touching of their infants at the first observation before discharge ($p < .05$), and spent more time smiling at their infants before discharge, 1 week, and 1 month after discharge ($p < .01$ at each observation), and at 11 months after discharge ($p < .05$) than did mothers of prematures. Full-term mothers also were higher in holding their infants close to their bodies than were mothers of prematures through 6 months after discharge.

Infant Development

Using the Bayley scales, full-term infants consistently scored higher than prematures in mental and motor development, even when computing the ''age'' of the prematures as months since discharge, which closely approximates what their age would have been had they been carried to term. There were no differences between the two groups of prematures. Social class was positively related to mental scores at 21 months after discharge, but not before. No other differences were found in mental and motor development except that, as noted earlier, maternal self-confidence at 1 month was related to increases in mental scores between discharge and 3 months later.

Other Findings

Although self-confidence was the only outcome measure in the study design which demonstrated significant effects of the separation experience, other observations made by the research team suggest that the Separation group may have otherwise been adversely affected. Two mothers in each of the two groups of prematures attempted to breast feed their infants. In both groups one was a primiparous mother, the other a multiparous mother who had successfully breast-fed an earlier child. The only mother who was successful with her premature infant was the multiparous mother in the Contact group. The second finding was that during the 15 months following discharge, six sets of parents separated and later divorced. Of these, five were in the Separation group. Surprisingly, particularly given the time of the study, two of the mothers in the Separation group voluntarily gave up custody at the time of the divorce. These findings suggest that mothers or parents in the Separation group were more stressed by the experience of separation and/or prematurity than those in the Contact group. From the information we had available, the differential divorce rates could not be accounted for by differences in the earlier marital relationship, social class, or by the sex, birth order, or general health of the infant.

COMPARABILITY TO OTHER RESEARCH

The intervention strategy in this study was very similar to that used by Kennell, Gordon, and Klaus with mothers of premature infants (see Klaus & Kennell, 1970), and shared some of the same theoretical assumptions as other studies of early contact among full-term mothers (Kennell, Jerauld, Wolfe, Chester, Kreger, McAlpine, Steffa, & Klaus, 1974; Klaus, Jerauld, Kreger, McAlpine, Steffa, & Kennell, 1972; Klaus & Kennell, 1976). Our findings are not consistent with those of Kennell et al., probably because of differences in the samples and the conditions of study. Our mothers, in contrast to those in their study, were predominantly white, middle-class, married, and living with their husbands at the time of the study. In addition, by virtue of their continuing contact with the members of the research group, all mothers in our study were given considerable psychological support throughout the first 2 years, although it had not been our intention to serve this function. There may also have been differences between the two studies in the mothers' experiences with hospital personnel and procedures, although we have no data with which to support or test this possibility. In our study other factors such as parity, sex of the infant, and social class were as important in determining later behavior as the separation experience.

  Some, but by no means all, of the outcome measures used in our study have been used in other studies of mothers and infants, although not necessarily in studies of separation. Use of the Maternal Attitude Scale has been reported by Tulkin and Cohler (1973), and a number of researchers have subsequently used our self-confidence scale, although results of their studies have not yet been published to my knowledge. Our assessments of interview data are similar to those reported by Moss and Jones (1977), although we did not analyze these data as extensively or in quite the same way. Nevertheless, both studies used similar information in assessing the mother's attitudes toward her infant.

The methods of measuring a mother's attachment behavior toward her infant in our study are very similar both in basic technique and variables to those reported by Klaus and Kennell (1976), Moss and Jones (1977) and by Yarrow, Pedersen, and Rubinstein (1977). There are, however, major differences in the timing and length of observations made in each study, with the length varying from 10 minutes to 6 hours.

The Bayley Scales of Infant Development and weight gain have each been used in numerous studies of infant development and do not seem to be a major area of divergence. Studies do differ, however, in the time and frequency of testing. As noted earlier, we had to use raw scores rather than Bayley's developmental quotients because of our focus on premature infants. This makes it difficult to make some comparison across studies, although comparisons of findings on group differences could be made.

DIRECTIONS FOR FUTURE RESEARCH

The conclusions that can be drawn from most of the past research on the effects of intervention in the neonatal period on mothers and infants are severely limited by the sizes of the samples and the resulting restrictions on the number of variables that can be considered. One of the most important findings from our research as well as that of others is the multiplicity of factors that appear to influence maternal attitudes, maternal behavior, and infant development, and the apparent inconsistency of the significance of these relationships over time.

The findings of Tulkin (1977) and of Moss and Jones (1977) among others on the influence of social class on maternal attitudes, maternal behavior, and the relationship between the two suggest that social class must be taken into account when using these variables to assess outcome. The same is true for the early initial state of the infant and the obstetric medications given to mothers according to the findings of Richards (1977). Birth order and sex of infants are also known to influence attitudes and behavior. At a minimum, we need to measure and report these variables in order to interpret research findings and particularly differences from one study to the next. A far better means of controlling for these factors is to study large enough samples to allow for multivariate statistical analysis. One of the findings in our study was that differences that appeared significant using analysis of variance or t tests were not significant when other variables were taken into account in multiple regression analysis.

I do not think that we are yet ready to, or need to, come to agreement on intervention strategies, particularly given the limitations of past research mentioned previously. It is important, however, to evaluate the effects of intervention in light of the total experience of the mother and infant while in the hospital. Not only have we studied different populations, but they have been in different hospital environments, which may facilitate or diminish the effects of intervention.

In assessing outcome, there should be some agreement or at least discussion on the relative merits of different measures. Where, as in the case of maternal attachment behaviors, there already seem to be significant commonalities in assessment techniques, the differences in timing and duration of observation unnecessarily complicate interpretation of the comparability of findings. It may be that it is possible to come to some agreement as to the timing of these observations, or as to what differences are likely to arise due to differences in the scheduling of observations. The differences in the duration of observations, from 10 minutes to 6 hours, are so great as to suggest that agreement on optimum duration is unlikely, particularly in terms of practicality. It would, however, seem possible to assess the impact of the length of the observation by looking at behavior over a short period of time within the longer observations. This may not, however, compensate for differences in the setting or in the relationship established between the mother and the observer.

One of the problems in interpreting results from past research, which this conference can compensate for in part, is incomplete information on the characteristics of the sample and also information on other measures which may have been included but have not been reported because of the inconclusiveness of the results. Only by sharing this information, and perhaps reviewing some of our own data, can we determine the relative utility, reliability, and validity of various measures.

If we are to come to some agreement on outcome assessment measures, then careful attention needs to be given to selecting those measures that are simple to interpret as well as useful. We had the greatest problems in interpreting results from our own research when we were dealing with summary measures, particularly from questionnaire data where it was difficult to determine the relative weight of various components. This is more a cautionary note than a criticism of past research in this area, because findings generally have been reported in the form of both summary scores and individual items. Because interview data have generally been more useful than responses to questionnaires, more information needs to be given on both the questions asked and specific coding procedures used. This is perhaps too cumbersome for article length presentations, but arrangements could and should be made for making such information available to others doing research in the same area.

In summary, the most important directions appear to be in increasing the size and heterogeneity of samples, particularly so that families from differing social classes and ethnic backgrounds as well as male and female infants are included. A case can be made at this stage for concentrating on primiparous mothers because they are the most likely to be influenced by any intervention, but this should be a temporary phase. Greater theoretical and methodological consideration also needs to be given to the variety of factors other than intervention strategy that may influence outcome.

It would clearly be valuable to have greater agreement, at least on the timing, of outcome measures. The greater the similarity in the actual measures used, the more agreement we can reach as to the relative effectiveness of various intervention strategies.

Although it is not necessarily an issue of either comparability or generalizability, greater emphasis should be placed on longitudinal studies of the effects of neonatal intervention, at least with a randomly selected subsample of the study group. To demonstrate that a given manipulation makes a difference at 1 or even 6 months is interesting, and may be clinically important, but the longer term consequences should also be studied. These are the true tests of the significance of an intervention or experience. Longitudinal studies dictate increased sample size, both because of problems with attrition and the increased diversity in the experiences of those in the sample over time, which may influence outcome. The need for larger samples suggests that areas of collaboration should be explored. The greatest need, however, is in maintaining communication about the details of research in this area, and coordinating efforts and procedures wherever feasible.

ACKNOWLEDGMENTS

Funding for the research by Leiderman and Barnett et al. was provided by grants from the Grant Foundation, New York, from the National Institute of Child Health and Human Development (Grant HD–02636), and from the National Institute of Mental Health (Grant MH 20162 05 Al).

REFERENCES

Ainsworth, M. D. The effects of maternal deprivation: A review of findings and controversy in the context of research strategy. *In Deprivation of maternal care: A reassessment of its effects*. Public Health Paper No. 14. Geneva: World Health Organization, 1962.

Barnett, C. R., Leiderman, P. H., Grobstein, R., & Klaus, M. H. Neonatal separation: The maternal side of interactional deprivation. *Pediatrics*, 1970, *45*, 197–205.

Bayley, N. *Bayley scales of infant development*. New York: Psychological Corp., 1969.

Bibring, G., Dwyer, T. F., Huntington, D. S., & Valenstein, A. F. A study of the psychological processes in pregnancy and the earliest mother–child relationship. *Psychoanalytic Study of the Child*, 1961, *16*, 9–27.

Bowlby, J., Ainsworth, M. D., Boston, M., & Rosenbluth, D. The effects of mother–child separation: A follow-up study. *British Journal of Medical Psychology*, 1956, *29*, 211–247.

Kennell, J. H., Jerauld, R., Wolfe, H., Chesler, D., Kreger, N. C., McAlpine, W., Steffa, M., & Klaus, M. H. Maternal behavior one year after early and extended post-partum contact, *Developmental Medicine and Child Neurology*, 1974, *16*, 172–179.

Klaus, M. H., Jerauld, R., Kreger, N. C., McAlpine, W., Steffa, M., & Kennell, J. H. Maternal attachment: Importance of the first post-partum days. *New England Journal of Medicine,* 1972, *281,* 460-463.

Klaus, M. H., & Kennell, J. H. Mothers separated from their newborn infants. *The Pediatric Clinics of North America,* 1970, *17,* 1015-1037.

Klaus, M. H., & Kennell, J. H. *Maternal-infant bonding: The impact of early separation or loss on family development.* St. Louis: C. V. Mosby, 1976.

Klopfer, P. H., Adams, D. K., & Klopfer, M. S. Maternal "imprinting" in goats. *Proceedings of the National Academy of Sciences,* 1964, *52,* 911-914.

Leiderman, P. H. The critical period hypothesis revisited: Mother to infant social bonding in the neonatal period. In F. Horowitz (Ed.), *Early developmental hazards: Predictors and precautions.,* Boulder, Colo.: Westview Press, Inc., 1978.

Leiderman, P. H., Leifer, A. D., Seashore, M. J., Barnett, C. R., & Grobstein, R. Mother-infant interaction: Effects of early deprivation, prior experience and sex of infant. In J. I. Nurnberger (Ed.), *Biological and environmental determinants of early development,* ARNMD (Vol. 51). Baltimore: Williams & Wilkins, 1973.

Leiderman, P. H., & Seashore, M. J. Mother-infant separation: Some delayed consequences. In *Ciba Foundation Symposium No. 33: Parent-infant interaction.* Amsterdam: Elsevier, 1975.

Leifer, A. D., Leiderman, P. H., Barnett, C. R., & Williams, J. A. Effects of mother-infant separation on maternal attachment behavior. *Child Development,* 1972, *43,* 1203-1218.

Moore, A. U. Effects of modified maternal care in the sheep and goat. In G. Newton & S. Levine (Eds.), *Early experience and behavior.* Springfield, Ill.: Charles C Thomas, 1968.

Moss, H. A. Sex, age and state as determinants of mother-infant interaction. *Merrill-Palmer Quarterly,* 1967, *13,* 19-36.

Moss, H. A., & Jones, S. J. Relations between maternal attitudes and maternal behavior as a function of social class. In P. H. Leiderman, S. R. Tulkin, & A. Rosenfeld (Eds.), *Culture and infancy: Variations in the human experience.* London: Academic Press, 1977.

Noirot, E. Changes in responsiveness to young in the adult mouse: The effect of external stimuli. *Journal of Comparative and Physiological Psychology,* 1964, *57,* 97-99.

Richards, M. P. M. An ecological study of infant development in an urban setting in Britain. In P. H. Leiderman, S. R. Tulkin, & A. Rosenfeld (Eds.), *Culture and infancy: Variations in the human experience.* London: Academic Press, 1977.

Robson, K. The role of eye-to-eye contact in maternal infant attachment. *Journal of Child Psychology and Psychiatry,* 1967, *8,* 13.

Rosenblatt, J. S., & Lehrman, D. S. Maternal behavior of the laboratory rat. In H. Rheingold (Ed.), *Maternal behavior in mammals.* New York: Wiley, 1963.

Seashore, M. J., Leifer, A. D., Barnett, C. R., & Leiderman, P. H. The effects of denial of early mother-infant interaction on maternal self-confidence. *Journal of Personality and Social Psychology,* 1973, *26,* 369-378.

Spitz, R. A. Unhappy and fatal outcomes of emotional deprivation and stress in infancy. In I. Galdston (Ed.), *Beyond the germ theory.* New York: Health Education Council, 1954.

Tulkin, S. R. Social class differences in maternal and infant behavior. In P. H. Leiderman, S. R. Tulkin, & A. Rosenfeld (Eds.), *Culture and infancy: Variations in the human experience.* London: Academic Press, 1977.

Tulkin, S. R. & Cohler, B. J. Child-rearing attitudes and mother-child interaction in the first year of life. *Merrill-Palmer Quarterly,* 1973, *19,* 95-106.

Warner, W. L., Meeker, M., & Ells, K. *Social class in America.* Chicago: Science Research Associates, 1949.

Yarrow, L. J., Pedersen, F. A., & Rubenstein, J. Mother-infant interaction and development in infancy. In P. H. Leiderman, S. R. Tulkin, &A. Rosenfeld (Eds.), *Culture and infancy: Variations in the human experience.* London: Academic Press, 1977.

9 Parent-Infant Bonding: Nature of Intervention and Inferences from Data

Michael W. Yogman
Harvard Medical School
and
Children's Hospital Medical Center

The research summarized by Drs. Trause and Seashore has had a powerful impact on hospital policies. This work has highlighted the inadequacy of rigid hospital policies, which restrict the right of a mother and father to be with their baby if they so desire. Given the enormous impact of these studies in fostering ongoing changes in the ecology of perinatal care in hospitals, the time is now appropriate to take a broad look at the many studies of early mother–infant contact and to consider directions for future research in this area (Klaus, Jerauld, Kreger, McAlpine, Steffa, & Kennell, 1972; Klaus & Kennell, 1976). Therefore, it seems useful at this point to consider the empirical data, the inferences drawn from these studies, and the generalizability of the results to an individual mother about to deliver a baby.

This chapter focuses on two different issues. The first issue is methodological and concerns the multifaceted nature of the intervention variable manipulated in these studies. The second issue concerns the range of inferences that can be drawn from these results. Future research in this area must formulate and test alternative hypotheses so that eventually the underlying processes of the early mother–infant relationship are better understood and can be optimally translated into clinical practice.

METHODOLOGY

First of all, the nature of any intervention with parents in the neonatal period may be perceived very differently by experimenters, by nursing staff, and by mothers. What are these different perceptions, how do they define the nature of the intervention, and what aspects of the intervention are responsible for the results? Whereas most of the studies have considered and varied the timing and duration of the mother's physical contact with her baby, no one has discussed in a detailed way the nature of the hospital milieu. In the Cleveland studies of full-term infants (Klaus & Kennell, 1976), mothers receiving early contact could compare their treatment to that of other mothers in adjoining rooms, and therefore must have known they were receiving special attention. The same nurses cared for both experimental and control mothers. Yet these nurses may have considered experimental mothers to be special, because these nurses were instructed to offer the experimental mothers a new and innovative opportunity for interaction with their babies, whereas with control mothers they offered routine care. Although unaware that they were acting differently, could these nurses have transmitted different messages to the mothers in these two groups? Could their expectations have influenced the babies as well? I suggest that, given what the studies of Rosenthal and colleagues (Rosenthal & Fode, 1963; Rosenthal & Lawson, 1964) have shown us about the subtlety and power of the expectancy effect in any experiment, the nurses may have differentially influenced the mothers. In fact, Rosenthal has shown that the effect persists not only in the absence of verbal communication, but is even present across species. He describes studies of a strain of pure-bred laboratory rats randomly labeled smart and dumb the night before they were to run a T-maze. Because the rats performed according to expectations, he postulated that the handling by experimenters was shaped by their expectations and differentially influenced the rats' performance.

Although the situation in Dr. Seashore's studies in the intensive care nursery is somewhat different, the same effect may operate. One suspects that the nursing staff of the Stanford Intensive Care Nursery may have acted somewhat differently toward the parents during the alternate 3-month periods when parents were allowed to visit the nursery and were, therefore, special. Given the present studies, it is difficult to specify that the intervention is merely extended contact; the implementation of this effect may change the hospital milieu and alter the way certain mothers and babies are treated. Findings such as Dr. Seashore's on enhanced maternal self-confidence are perfectly compatible with this possibility.

What is needed, I believe, is more precise documentation of the nature of the effective intervention. How is the intervention described to parents to enlist their consent, how is it introduced to them at the time of intervention, what do they understand about it, and how is the potential disappointment dealt with in the control group? One valuable technique might be to share videotapes of the intervention with investigators outside the project so that independent descriptions of the intervention can be compared.

The rationale for interventions in different situations needs to be distinguished. With healthy, full-term babies, early contact may enable a mother to see her baby in an alert state; with preterm infants, encouraging mothers to visit the high-risk nursery may aid in resolution of their normal grief reaction, independent of actual contact with the baby. Even if current hospital practices interfere with the needs of healthy mothers and babies, these violations are far less than the distortions that accompany premature birth. Although the importance of visiting has been emphasized, probably the impact on the mother depends most on what happens when she actually visits. Does the baby have a primary nurse? How supportive are the interactions between mother and nurses and doctors, apart from whether the mother is allowed to hold her baby? Nursery staff members themselves can get very attached to these babies, and that can generate competition with parents rather than support. Replication of studies such as those in Cleveland or Stanford will require the same sensitivity to these aspects of the intervention, or else the results will not be strictly comparable. One of the benefits of these studies is that by opening up nurseries to parents, the entire milieu is changed. This may explain why Dr. Seashore had difficulties demonstrating differences between the contact and separation groups in her studies. Perhaps future studies should document the effect of interventions, not only on parents, but on the staff of the nursery as well.

Not only do we need to understand the nature of the intervention, but we need to understand its specificity: In which families does it have the greatest influence? The studies in the United States and Guatemala (Klaus & Kennell, 1976) show that early contact has an effect on low-income mothers. Is the documented effect for these mothers one of specifically enhancing mother–infant bonding, or does it improve maternal self-esteem and indirectly enhance maternal care? Answers to such questions are critical to issues such as generalizability. Studies of middle-class populations in Sweden by de Chateau and Wiberg (1977) have begun to answer the first question, but answers to the second question will require other experimental designs. A better understanding of the interaction of the intervention with variables such as complications of labor, maternal fatigue, and newborn behavior is required so that we can better understand both the universal impact of these interventions and the ways in which they can be individualized.

INFERENCES FROM THE DATA

Given the results of the effectiveness of perinatal interventions and their implications for clinical practice, what inferences can be drawn for our theoretical understanding of early infant social development? The accumulating data documenting the profound effect of these interventions lead one to ask *why* these interventions are effective. Here the question is not one of the comparability of the findings in different settings, but is a question that requires a different research strategy. The goal here is to elucidate the mechanism of this effect, to understand the process of mother–infant interaction in the newborn period, and to understand how it influences later cognitive and emotional development.

On the basis of cross-phylogenetic and ethnographic data, Klaus and Kennell (1976) suggest that the effect of the intervention indicates the existence of a maternal "sensitive period." Since this term was first used, the distinctions between 'sensitive'' and ''critical period'' have become increasingly blurred. I do not think the data necessarily support the inference that a limited period exists in humans during which bonding takes place in an all-or-none fashion. All that we know of human behavior suggests that humans are too resilient for such a constraint to be absolute and that development is a much more dynamic interactional process, both between the infant and the caregiver and between maturational forces and environmental ones. It is certainly true that medical care and hospital policies toward childbirth have distorted and transformed it from a normal event to a medical disease. These studies of early contact may be a powerful reminder of just how much of a violation current medical practices have become for many families. However, one must be cautious when extrapolating from the effects of interventions in a violated system to postulating the existence of a ''sensitive period'' for bonding in a nonviolated system.

Clearly, the ''sensitive period'' hypothesis is only one of several alternative interpretations of the data. Is the perinatal period only a ''sensitive'' period for early contact or is it also a ''sensitive'' period in a more general sense for parents who have just had a baby? The entire perinatal period may be an opportune time for intervention merely because of the shifts in organization in the family. Bibring's (1959) studies of pregnancy have documented this upheaval in which old bonds are loosened as mothers re-integrate their roles of daughter and wife with that of mother. Such studies, as well as clinical experiences in our training program at Children's Hospital in which pediatricians interview mothers prenatally, suggest that mothers are particularly available to intervention during the entire perinatal period for psychological as well as physiological reasons. For example, after birth a mother probably has a heightened awareness of people who think she is ''special.'' When a mother is isolated in an impersonal hospital environment, she is probably more available to any intervention with personal, human contact that conveys the message that she is ''special.''

Given the disequilibrium in the family at this time, the effectiveness of any intervention is likely to depend not only how ready the individual mother is to re-integrate her roles and form new bonds, but also on how responsive and eliciting the baby is. It has been suggested that one reason for the effectiveness of early contact is that newborns have a period of quiet alertness during the first hour after birth (Desmond, Franklin, Vallbona, Hill, Plumb, Arnold, & Watts, 1963), which is more prolonged than at other times during the first week. How does the quality of newborn alertness influence bonding, and can other interventions be implemented so as to coincide with subsequent periods of newborn alertness? For instance, could the feeding and handling of premature infants by parents and nurses be done during alert periods throughout the hospitalization experience? Because the goal of intervention is an optimal fit between mother and baby, does early contact always facilitate the fit between a mother who expects a placid, calm baby and gets a fussy, irritable one, or does this situation require allowing the mother to define the time and proximity she wants with her baby? How is the process modified when the mother delivers a baby that has a low birthweight? Premature and small for gestational age babies (Als, Tronick, Adamson, & Brazelton, 1976) may behave very differently during early contact. If we agree that the parent's goal is to establish a situation of continuing reciprocal stimulation leading to the formation of a (long-term) social bond (Tobach & Schneirla, 1968), then we must think in terms of the availability of both mother and infant to engage in ongoing reciprocal stimulation. Variables such as childbirth education, which has been shown to influence maternal medication and the type of delivery (Scott & Rose, 1976), become important not only because they influence the fetus, but because they affect the mother post partum and influence her alertness, her feelings of control and confidence, and in turn, her receptivity to an intervention.

Demonstrating to a mother her newborn's behavioral capacities (Brazelton, 1973) may be another way to facilitate the early mother–infant relationship. As an intervention, this can be used not only with mother and baby, but with father and other caretakers as well. Using neonatal behavior in this way is likely to influence the professional who interacts with the baby and the professional's later relationship with the parents almost as much as it may influence the parents themselves.

Assessing a newborn in this way allows a more individualized approach to intervention. With term newborns, demonstrations of newborn behavior can help parents to identify optimal periods of alertness for interaction with their baby and optimal amounts and timing of stimulation. With preterm newborns, observing their baby's behavior may help parents to see their baby as a person and shift the focus from questions of survival once it is appropriate. The mother of a preterm infant who had seen her baby look up and brighten, for the briefest period, described the episode as: "Thrilling, just what I needed; now I know he's okay and he's mine." For preterm parents about to take their baby home from the hospital, this experience may facilitate the transition from delegating the care of one's baby to doctors and nurses to assuming full responsibility for care of one's own baby.

Given the stresses of current medical and cultural practices, maternal bonding may be more difficult in the absence of early contact, but it surely can and does take place for mothers of sick preterm infants, for mothers delivering by Caesarean section, and for adoptive mothers. Overinterpretation of the data about the importance of early contact during the "sensitive period" could reinforce feelings of self-doubt in these parents and add an unfair burden of guilt. There is simply no evidence that early contact is essential for optimal development. In fact, Macfarlane (1977) has suggested that in an evolutionary sense, there may be some adaptive value for parents to postpone attachment to their baby until they are reasonably certain of survival.

Only by a better understanding of the underlying process of early attachment will it be feasible to document not only significant group effects of blanket interventions but also significant effects on individuals of interventions that are modified to specifically fit each person. We can often learn as much by intensively studying interventions in single families as we can from group studies. We need to recognize that mother's first response to her infant is not always positive. In the Robson and Moss (1970) study, women described feelings of strangeness and unfamiliarity with their babies for several weeks. These feelings are not only normal, but are probably adaptive for allowing the eventual development of autonomy.

Finally, as part of this effort to understand the effects of interventions on the early parent–infant relationship, we must broaden our look at the social world of newborns and infants. Trause (Trause, Boslett, Voos, Rudd, Kennell, & Klaus, 1977) has done a study of the important effects childbirth has on siblings between 1 and 3 years of age. A Swedish investigator named Johannesson (1969) has shown that simply instructing fathers in child care—bathing, changing, and feeding—on two evenings in the hospital is associated with their greater participation in infant care 6 weeks later. Greenberg and Morris (1974) suggest that a father's feelings of involvement may be enhanced if fathers are present during delivery.

Again, the data should not be overinterpreted. Fein's (1976) studies suggest that the most effective postpartum adjustment for fathers does not seem to be related simply to high involvement, but rather to a more coherent integration of roles by mother and father. Studies of father–infant and mother–infant interaction and reciprocity give us some insights into how this negotiation occurs and how early attachments occur within the family system (Earles & Yogman, 1979; Yogman, 1977). We have noticed that the games fathers play with their infants have a more excited and heightened quality than those of mothers. Such successful interactions may help fathers to think of themselves as special and unique and may offer infants a different and yet complementary interactive experience than occurs with mothers. Can researchers begin to think about the bonding of infants within a family framework so that fathers are systematically included rather than added as an appendage?

In summary, the studies described at this conference have had a dramatic impact on opening up hospitals and improving family care. The task for future research is to understand the underlying process of parent–infant bonding so that clinicians can apply that understanding to individual families.

REFERENCES

Als, H., Tronick, E., Adamson, L., & Brazelton, T. B. The behavior of the full-term underweight newborn. *Developmental Medicine and Child Neurology,* 1976, *18,* 590–602.

Bibring, G. Some considerations of the psychological processes in pregnancy. *Psychoanalytic Study of the Child,* 1959, *14,* 113.

Brazelton, T. B. Neonatal behavioral assessment scale. *Clinics in Developmental Medicine,* (No. 50). Philadelphia: J. P. Lippincott, 1973.

de Chateau, P., & Wiberg, B. Long-term effect on mother–infant behavior of extra contact during the first hour post partum. I. First observations at 36 hours. *Acta Paediatrica Scandinavia, 1977, 66,* 137–143.

Desmond, M. M., Franklin, R. R., Vallbona, C., Hill, R. M., Plumb, R., Arnold, H., & Watts, J. The clinical behavior of the newly born. I. The term baby. *Journal of Pediatrics, 1963, 62,* 307–325.

Earles, F., & Yogman, M. The father-infant relationship. In J. Howells (Ed.), *Modern perspectives in the psychiatry of infancy.* New York: Brunner/Mazel, 1979.

Fein, R. A. Men's entrance to parenthood. *Family Coordinator, 1976, 25,* 341.

Greenberg, M., & Morris, N. Engrossment: The newborn's impact upon the father. *American Journal of Orthopsychiatry, 1974, 44,* 520–531.

Johannesson, P. W. *Instruction in child care for fathers.* Unpublished doctoral dissertation, University of Stockholm, 1969.

Klaus, M., Jerauld, R., Kreger, N., McAlpine, W., Steffa, M. & Kennell, J. H. Maternal attachment: Importance of the first post-partum days. *New England Journal of Medicine, 1972, 286,* 460–463.

Klaus, M., & Kennell, J. *Maternal–infant bonding.* St. Louis: Mosby, 1976.

Macfarlane, A. *The psychology of childbirth.* Cambridge: Harvard University Press, 1977.

Robson, K. S., & Moss, H. A. Patterns and determinants of maternal attachment. *Journal of Pediatrics, 1970, 77,* 976–985.

Rosenthal, R., & Fode, K. L. The effect of experimenter bias on the performance of the albino rat. *Behavioral Science, 1963, 8,* 183–189.

Rosenthal, R., & Lawson, R. A longitudinal study of the effects of experimenter bias on operant learning in laboratory rats. *Journal of Psychiatric Research, 1964, 2,* 61.

Scott, J., & Rose, N. Effect of psychoprophylaxis (Lamaze preparation) on labor and delivery in primiparas. *New England Journal of Medicine, 1976, 294,* 1205–1207.

Tobach, E., & Schneirla, T. C. The biopsychology of social behavior in animals. In R. Cooke (Ed.), *The biologic basis of pediatric practice,* New York: McGraw Hill, 1968.

Trause, M. A., Boslett, M., Voos, D., Rudd, C., Kennell, J., & Klaus, M. *A birth in the hospital: The effect on the sibling.* Paper presented at the meeting of the Society for Pediatric Research, San Francisco, April 1977.

Yogman, M. The goals and structure of face-to-face interaction between infants and fathers. Paper presented at the meeting of the Society for Research in Child Development, New Orleans, March 1977.

10

Effects of Mother–Newborn Contact: Comparability and Validity of Measures

Vincent L. Smeriglio
Johns Hopkins University

SIMILARITIES AND DIFFERENCES IN CURRENTLY USED MEASURES

As the papers by Trause and Seashore indicate, comparisons across studies reveal similarities and differences in measures used to assess effects of mother–newborn contact. Most studies report some index of maternal "attachment" behaviors based on observations of mother–infant interactions (for examples, see de Chateau & Wiberg, 1977a, 1977b; Kontos, 1978; see papers by Trause and Seashore in this volume). Although there is similarity in what is being observed, as Seashore points out in her paper, the differences in timing and duration of observation complicate comparison of findings. Despite these limitations, the similarity of observation procedures and the common interest in this dimension of effect suggest potential for agreement on measures of maternal "attachment" behaviors. In fact, there already is evidence of collaboration on measures of maternal behaviors—as for example between the Trause, Kennell, and Klaus group in Cleveland and the de Chateau group in Umea, Sweden (de Chateau & Wiberg, 1977a).

Dissimilarity exceeds similarity when looking at outcome measures other than "attachment" behaviors. For example, the Stanford group (see Seashore paper) assessed maternal attitudes to a considerable degree with interviews and questionnaires; the Case Western Reserve group (see Trause paper) dealt briefly with what might be considered maternal attitudes or feelings in its interview questions. Some studies have reported on breastfeeding indices as outcome measures (e.g., de Chateau & Wiberg, 1977b; Sosa, Kennell, Klaus, & Urrutia, 1976). In other studies, measures of early contact effects have included infant development scores (e.g., Seashore, this volume), maternal linguistic behaviors (Ringler, Kennell, Jarvella, Navojosky, & Klaus, 1975), and indices of children's speech, language comprehension, and IQ (Ringler, Trause, Klaus, & Kennell, 1978).

VALUE OF AN EXPLICIT CONCEPTUAL FRAMEWORK FOR EXPECTED EFFECTS

If an increase in comparability of outcome measures is a desirable goal, then there must be a practical stimulus and a practical orienting mechanism to channel efforts toward that end. One possibility that potentially could provide such a stimulus and orienting mechanism is well within our traditional means of scientific communication. That possibility is for researchers to be explicit regarding postulated processes of intervention effects and areas of expected impact. What is being suggested is not necessarily precise hypothesis testing but simply consistent efforts toward more explicit expressions of conceptual framework for intervention effects. This conceptualization could be based on the child development literature as well as on clinical and research experiences of investigators.

Needless to say, the processes and effects cannot be known before the empirical work is done. But more explicit statements regarding conceptual framework for expected effects could lead to more consistent choice of measures, and consequently to a more systematic, unified approach to studying those processes and their effects. Furthermore, given the fact that research on mother–newborn contact is already an active and highly visible area, explicitly drawing attention to categories of possible effects could have the added benefit of stimulating much-needed development of new and valid measures.

For various reasons, explicit statements have occurred in the literature regarding the expectation that early mother–infant contact would promote heightened maternal ''attachment'' behaviors. Associated with such explicit expectations (although not necessarily a direct result of them) has been some commonality of approach to this assessment, with reasonable potential at present for increased comparability of ''attachment'' measures. What other dimensions of infant, child, and maternal functioning have a reasonable conceptual basis for expected impact? For example, if early contact influences the nature of the mother–infant relationship at one point in time (such as in the newborn period), should the nature of that relationship be expected to influence dimensions of child development at later points in time? If so, are the effects to be expected in the area of social functioning? Cognitive development? Why would the particular effects be expected? Our current base of empirical information regarding early experiences should allow for conceptualization on these and similar questions.

VALIDITY OF CURRENTLY USED
OUTCOME MEASURES

Of necessity, many of the currently used outcome measures rely on assumed rather than proven validity. Validated measures simply are not available for several of the effects of interest. Consequently, the conclusions drawn from the data must be cautious. For example, the fact that mothers in an extra-contact group demonstrate more smiling or en face looking (relative to those in a routine contact group) does not allow us to draw conclusions about the nature of their future mother–child relationships or about future child development. As Mary Anne Trause pointed out in her paper, at present we do not even have data to confirm that such measures as en face looking are in fact indices of maternal "attachment."

As one additional example of the limitations on validity of maternal "attachment" measures, consider the measure involving observations of maternal behaviors during a physical examination of the infant (e.g., see Klaus & Kennell, 1976). If during the exam a mother stands, watches, and soothes the infant's crying, such behavior is taken as evidence of a higher level of attachment relative to a mother who remains seated while watching the exam and who rarely soothes the infant's crying during the exam. The fact that data indicate a higher "attachment" score in the extra-contact group (e.g., see Klaus & Kennell, 1976) indeed could be evidence of a greater degree of attachment. But other interpretations are also plausible, as for example: Mothers in the experimental group learned via the extra-contact experience to feel more a part of their infants' medical care routines and to be more comfortable in the hospital and other health-care settings. Although such an outcome may be desirable, it does not necessarily reflect "attachment" to the infant.

Measures other than "attachment" behaviors have varying validity. For example, if for nutrition purposes the specific goal of intervention is to influence breastfeeding practices (e.g., to increase the number of mothers breastfeeding and the duration of breastfeeding), then conclusions based on such outcome measures are clear-cut. However, any inferences about later mother–child relationships as a result of data on these measures should be much more cautious. Use of infant development scales are subject to the usual concerns regarding predictive validity (e.g., Honzik, 1976).

It is possible that existing data would enable some validity analyses of currently used measures. One type of analysis that would appear worthwhile involves testing predictive validity of measures used within longitudinal studies, namely within the projects of the Case Western Reserve group (e.g., Trause paper in this volume), the Stanford group (e.g., Seashore paper in this volume), and the de Chateau group in Sweden (e.g., de Chateau & Wiberg, 1977b). For example, scores on measures of "attachment" used in the early part of the 1st year could be correlated with scores on later measures (such as later maternal behaviors, infant developmental performance, and childhood IQ). With few exceptions (e.g., Seashore paper in this volume; Seashore, Leifer, Barnett, & Leiderman, 1973; Ringler et al., 1978), analyses of this type have not been reported in the literature. What has been typical in longitudinal studies is reporting of experimental-control group comparisons at each assessment period. Although the suggested analyses would have limitations (such as those imposed by statistical considerations), they could capitalize on existing data to provide preliminary insight into predictive validity of some outcome measures.

Another type of validity analysis of existing data could involve determining whether individual mothers demonstrate clustering of behaviors assumed to reflect "attachment." For example, is a high level of en face looking associated with a high level of holding, touching, and other "attachment" behaviors? Most studies in the literature report experimental-control differences on a composite "attachment" index or on selected "attachment" behaviors separately. Once again, the suggested analyses would be subject to limitations but may give preliminary information as to some aspects of validity.

In conclusion, comparisons across studies reveal similarities and differences in measures currently employed to assess outcomes of mother–infant contact. These measures are of limited validity, and consequently conclusions drawn from the data require appropriate caution. Existing data possibly could be analyzed in ways to provide preliminary insight into some validity issues. Increased comparability in use of outcome measures as well as development of new measures may be enhanced by increased efforts toward explicit conceptualization for expected effects of mother–newborn contact.

REFERENCES

de Chateau, P., & Wiberg, B. Long-term effect on mother–infant behavior of extra contact during the first hour post partum. I. First observations at 36 hours. *Acta Paediatrica Scandanavia*, 1977, *66*, 137–143. (a)

de Chateau, P., & Wiberg, B. Long-term effect on mother–infant behavior of extra contact during the first hour post partum. II. A follow-up at three months. *Acta Paediatrica Scandanavia*, 1977, *66*, 145–151. (b)

Honzik, M. P. Value and limitations of infant tests: An overview. In M. Lewis (Ed.), *Origins of intelligence*. New York: Plenum Press, 1976.

Klaus, M. H., & Kennell, J. H. *Maternal–infant bonding*. St. Louis: C. V. Mosby, 1976.

Kontos, D. A study of the effects of extended mother–infant contact on maternal behavior at one and three months. *Birth and the Family Journal*, 1978, *5*, 133–140.

Ringler, N. M., Kennell, J. H., Jarvella, R., Navojosky, B. J., & Klaus, M. H. Mother-to-child speech at 2 years—Effects of early postnatal contact. *Journal of Pediatrics*, 1975, *86*, 141–144.

Ringler, N. M., Trause, M. A., Klaus, M. H., & Kennell, J. H. The effects of extra postpartum contact and maternal speech patterns on children's IQs, speech, and language comprehension at five. *Child Development*, 1978, *49*, 862–865.

Seashore, M. J., Leifer, A. D., Barnett, C. R., & Leiderman, P. H. The effects of denial of early mother–infant interaction on maternal self-confidence. *Journal of Personality and Social Psychology,* 1973, *26,* 369–378.

Sosa, R., Kennell, J. H., Klaus, M., & Urrutia, J. J. The effect of early mother–infant contact on breastfeeding, infection and growth. In Ciba Symposium 45, *Breastfeeding and the Infant.* Amsterdam: Elsevier, 1976.

IV UNDERSTANDING NEWBORN SENSORY STIMULATION AND PARENT–INFANT CONTACT: ADDITIONAL CONSIDERATIONS

11 Maternal Attitudes During Pregnancy and Medication During Labor and Delivery: Methodological Considerations

Raymond K. Yang
University of Georgia

In many areas of psychological research, the mutual and interactive influences of one party on another have long been recognized (for example, small group social psychology and systems theories in family sociology). In research on child rearing, recognition of this mutual and interactive effect occurred at a conceptual level long before it became visible at the level of data collection procedures. In their classic study of child rearing, Sears, Maccoby, and Levin (1957) prefaced their presentation of data with the caveat that "child rearing practices can be viewed as both cause and effect", but chose not to "attempt to untangle these reciprocal relations." [p. 12]. It remained for Bell (1968) to chide his colleagues to a point where actual data collection strategies were generated demonstrating these reciprocal relations.

In studying neonatal, prenatal, and perinatal influences, we are faced with the same problem. We recognize that a system of reciprocal effects exists, but we lack the technological skills to assess those effects. These skills are particularly lacking when assessing prenatal influences. The maternal-fetal system is a remarkable interactive system. Yet, for many of us (including myself), our skills in approaching this area are so lacking that we often consider it not a part of our area of inquiry, but of medical physiology, endocrinology, or the like. Thus, the maternal-fetal system is not defined as a psychological relationship. It is seen as falling within the purview of a field other than psychology. Not until birth is that system assigned psychological status, being relabeled the *mother–infant* relation.

This hiatus separating the maternal-fetal from the mother–infant system has, I feel, been associated with (and perhaps responsible for) two diverse views of the newborn. The first and most common is to view the newborn as a beginning point. Here, congenital, and to an extent, genetic predispositions can be assessed—at least to the extent that they are not environmentally influenced. Certainly, it is most often the point at which the behavioral scientist starts to measure the organism's interaction with the environment.

We can also view the newborn as an end-point. It is the culmination of something started at conception. It is the criterion measure for the evaluation of pregnancy. It is the criterion for the evaluation of the effects of labor and delivery. To the extent that the evaluation is based on the newborn alone, both of these criteria represent an individual orientation. That is, all of the measures are obtained from the newborn alone. They assess the organism as a self-contained entity, exhibiting behaviors in its new environment as if it had mechanistic qualities, yielding to psychophysical description.

The fact that the dependent variables for measuring effective environmental manipulation are neonatal behaviors should not restrict our appreciation of the wide range of influencing (i.e., moderator, suppressor, confounding) factors that exist. All too often, however, this is the case, due to our inclination to consider the maternal-fetal system as distinct from the mother–infant relationship.

What I would like to do at this point is review a group of selected empirical studies. Some deal with traditional issues to the extent that they can be easily categorized into a general scheme of research. I am unsure where to place others. I deal with these exemplary studies as they touch on the earlier issues that I have mentioned: the newborn as beginning and as end, the individual versus systems orientation, and the maternal-fetal versus mother–infant relation as an expression of physiological and psychological perspectives.

OBSTETRIC MEDICATION AND NEONATAL BEHAVIOR

The literature examining the effects of obstetric medication and neonatal outcome fall into two large categories: First are those studies, clinical in nature, describing case histories or presenting summary statistics of clinical procedures. These studies are not characterized by an experimental design; hence, they lack methodological control, adequate sampling, and other features of empirical studies. The second category of studies are those designed to meet these shortcomings. They are more experimental and empirical, and are being conducted with greater frequency.

Stechler (1964) examined the effects of obstetric analgesia on newborn visual attention. Stechler's measure of obstetric analgesia took into account not only dosage size but also the time of administration of the drug. Dosage was categorized as either "heavy" or "normal." Time of administration was represented by differential ratings, with larger ratings being given to drugs administered closer to delivery. The measure of visual attention was the amount of time the infant spent looking at a schematic face, a single die, and a blank sheet of paper. Stechler found that the composite drug measure was negatively correlated with the amount of time spent looking at the visual stimuli and concluded that "states of alert attentiveness can be found to be related to a significant *independent variable,* in this case, drugs used during labor. [p. 316, italics added]"

In 1966, Kron, Stein, and Goddard examined the relation between obstetric sedation during labor and delivery and the sucking behavior of newborn infants. Their measure of newborn sucking had extensive instrumentation; rate, rhythmicity, amount, and pressure of sucking were measured. The sample was comprised of 20 newborns born to 20 predominantly multiparous mothers (21 years of age). What makes the Kron et al. study distinctive was their experimental-control design. An experimental group received 200 milligrams of sodium secobarbital in a slow intravenous injection administered when the mother was in active labor. The control group received no analgesia or anasthesia during labor and delivery. Regarding potential methodological confounding, Kron et al. noted that, "clinical considerations did not enter into the selection of mothers who were or were not to receive obstetric sedation. The groups were constituted by random sampling of uncomplicated obstetrical patients, and the mothers were not given the opportunity to elect or refuse the medication." [p. 1013]. The authors found large and statistically significant differences in sucking behavior between the experimental and control group. Across the first three days of life, newborns in the experimental group sucked one-third to slightly over one-half as much as infants in the control group. The effects of the drugs were without dispute.

Both of these studies are exemplary, not only because they clearly demonstrate the relation between drugs administered to the mother during labor and newborn behavior, but because the criterion behaviors fall within what we would consider a clinically normal range. Equally important, both of these studies reflect the difficulty of employing rigorous methodologies. Stechler concluded that he had located an independent–dependent variable relationship. In effect, he had found a relationship between an antecedent and consequent event. He had not demonstrated a causal relationship. Kron et al. (1966) had actually demonstrated an independent–dependent variable relationship between obstetric sedation and newborn behavior. In spite of the small sample of Kron et al., it is reasonable to expect that the study will not be replicated. Notwithstanding, these relationships between drugs and behavior are well known and well accepted.

PSYCHOLOGICAL STATE DURING PREGNANCY

There is a group of studies, perhaps less well accepted, that extend these considerations chronologically in time. This group of studies relate some aspect of the mother's psychological state during pregnancy to events during labor and delivery.

Davids, DeVault, and Talmadge (1961) examined the relation between a standardized anxiety measure administered during pregnancy and complications of labor and delivery. Forty-eight women were administered the Taylor Manifest

Anxiety Scale during their seventh month of pregnancy. Based on delivery room records, their deliveries were later classified as "normal," or "abnormal," or "complicated." Comparisons of the normal versus abnormal group yielded differences in anxiety scores that were statistically significant: Women experiencing abnormal deliveries had higher anxiety scores than those experiencing normal deliveries. Those experiencing normal deliveries had anxiety scores comparable to nonpregnant women responding to the Manifest Anxiety Scale.

Although Davids et al. described their sample as representative of clinical populations (normal intelligence; mean age of 25 years), two factors suggested that the sample might have been from more depriving circumstances. Of the 48 mothers, 23 were eventually classified as experiencing abnormal or complicated deliveries. Davids et al. also reported that the 7th month assessment was the first prenatal visit for the majority of mothers. Late prenatal visits and a very high proportion of complicated deliveries suggest that selective factors other than clinic attendance were operating.

McDonald, Gynther, and Christakos (1963) studied the relation between maternal anxiety at the beginning of the last trimester and gestational disorders, complications of delivery, and newborn abnormalities. Their sample was comprised of 86 low socioeconomic status women (mean age of 23 years). McDonald et al. found that women classified as having abnormal pregnancies or deliveries had significantly higher anxiety scores than those not so classified. The most frequent complications occurring during pregnancy included pre-eclampsia and bleeding during the last trimester; the most frequently occurring complications during labor and delivery included prolonged labor, prolapse of the umbilical cord, and premature rupture of the membranes. The authors speculated that maternal anxiety, induced by various mechanisms (the autonomic nervous system, hypothalamico-pituitary axis, and vasomotor system), could be manifested in newborn developmental anomalies or maternal abnormalities, irrespective of whether or not they affected the fetus.

In 1960, Ferreira examined the relation between two variables: maternal "fear of harming the baby" and "rejection of the pregnancy," and nurses' subjective ratings of newborn behavior in the nursery. Ferreira's measure of harming the baby and rejection of the pregnancy were constructed from items selected from the Parental Attitude Research Instrument (Schaefer & Bell, 1958). The mother responded to these items during the last month of pregnancy. Following delivery, nurses rated the infants on amount of crying, sleeping irritability, bowel movements, and feeding. The infants were rated as either "normal" or "deviant" for 5 continuous days while they were in the nursery. Ferreira classified as deviant any infant who for at least 2 of the 5 days had been rated as being deviant in any area. By this method, Ferreira classified 28 of 163 infants as deviant. Comparisons of mothers' fears of harming the baby and rejection of pregnancy, when divided on the basis of their infants classified as deviant or normal indicated the following: Mothers of infants classified as deviant scored significantly higher on fear of harming the baby than mothers of infants classified as normal; mothers of deviant infants did not differ in their rejection of the pregnancy from mothers of normal infants. Interestingly, Ferreira found no relation between deviants and length of labor or anesthesia.

The Davids et al., McDonald et al., and Ferreira studies are examples of research indicating that psychological responses to pregnancy, particularly those that can be construed as "negative" can precede "problems" during labor and delivery. These problems are also those traditionally classified as clinical. These types of studies extend the chronology of "important considerations" back into pregnancy.

EFFECTS BEYOND THE NEONATAL PERIOD

Just as a group of studies extends consideration back into pregnancy, another group of studies, perhaps smaller, also extends consideration forward. One example is a study conducted by Conway and Brackbill (1970). They examined the relation between obstetric medication and behavior during the neonatal period. "Potency" of medication during labor and delivery was measured by averaging the rankings of two obstetricians who ranked mothers on the type and amount of analgesics, anesthetics, and tranquilizers that each mother received. Measures of newborn behavior included the muscle tension, vision, and maturation subscales of the Graham Test, and a measure of orienting response extinction to repeated auditory stimulation. The Graham Test was administered at 2 and 5 days of age, and again at 4 weeks of age. The Bayley Mental and Motor Scales were also administered at 4 weeks of age. Conway and Brackbill found all of these measures to be correlated with the obstetricians' rankings of medication potency during labor and delivery. Essentially, medication potency was negatively related to the scale scores and positively correlated to the measure of orienting response extinction.

What was most impressive was Conway and Brackbill's findings that at 4 weeks of age, the infants' scores on the Bayley assessment were still significantly correlated with the ranking of potency of obstetric medication. Most intriguing was Conway and Brackbill's finding that even at 20 weeks of age, potency of obstetric medication was still related to extinction of the orienting reflex. Even at this age, high potency of medication was associated with greater numbers of trials to extinction of the orienting reflex.

More recently, Brackbill (1979a, 1979b) has reviewed a number of studies unanimously revealing effects of obstetric sedation on infant behavior. Brackbill argues that as a group these studies yield several provocative generalizations: (1) drug effects upon the infant were not transient, but may have persisted for 7 months in some of the studies; (2) drug effects on the infant (or young child) were most apparent when the assessments involved performance on difficult tasks (when the task did not involve sustained attention, coping, or intensive effort, drug effects often went undetected); and (3) the behavioral changes associated with obstetric medication did not appear to covary with other factors, e.g. prenatal risk or complications, parity, and socioeconomic status.

These findings and others reported by Brackbill and Broman have attracted considerable attention (e.g., Brackbill, 1979b; Broman, 1979; Kolata, 1978, 1979). In analyzing data from the National Institutes of Health Collaborative Perinatal Project, Brackbill and Broman argued that in a carefully selected subsample of mothers and infants with no detectable perinatal complications, dose-related effects of obstetric sedation could be found in the children as late as 7 years of age. These effects were most visible in lagging linguistic and cognitive skills. Reports in the public press of Brackbill and Broman's findings have attributed a "14 million IQ point" loss across 3.7 million births per year in the United States. Critics of Broman and Brackbill have raised questions about the selection of their samples and the adequacy of their statistical analyses. "Natural" childbirth advocates have rallied to Broman and Brackbill's defense. And, at least one observer had described the current situation as polarized and at an impasse (Kolata, 1979).

A LARGER PERSPECTIVE

Only empirical studies have been reviewed in this presentation. Case studies, groups of case studies, and clinical runs have not been included. Generally, the latter have not yielded information helpful in guiding normative procedures (Hellman & Pritchard, 1971). Notwithstanding, the empirical studies have been characterized by an overly selective focus, caused in part by the disciplinary boundary separating the physiological from the psychological. The possibility that maternal psychological functioning and obstetric sedation might covary and have mutual (or interactive) influences on the newborn and infant has not been dealt with.

In 1976, my colleagues and I tried to examine this issue (Yang, Zweig, Douthitt, & Federman, 1976). As a part of the Bethesda Longitudinal Study conducted at the National Institute of Mental Health, we had access to data describing the psychological state of the mother during her third trimester of pregnancy, and her newborn. Howard Moss, Thomas Douthitt, and Richard Bell directed the collection of those data. The psychological state of the mother during the last trimester was assessed through interviews and questionnaires. We drew a measure of anxiety from those assessments; the measure included fears regarding pregnancy as well as generalized depression, irritability, and tension. The newborn data was comprised of sleep and waking behavior measured across a standardized 5-hour assessment. During this assessment, active and quiet sleep were measured, as were heart and respiratory rate. In addition, stimuli were presented that elicited sucking and crying. Finally, standardized information regarding labor, delivery, and medication were obtained from hospital records.

We examined sequential relations between each set of data. What we feel we demonstrated were some common sense relations: maternal fears, irritability, depression, and tension, assessed during the last trimester of pregnancy, were positively correlated with the number of drugs administered to the mother during labor. The number of drugs administered during labor was positively correlated with the duration of labor (Stage I). The number of drugs administered the mother was negatively correlated with the 5-minute Apgar. We surmised that maternal anxiety during the last trimester was transformed into increased discomfort during labor. This in turn was responded to by medical staff in the form of increased medication. The increased medication, in turn, had the traditional depressive effect on the newborn.

This relationship between maternal attitudes during pregnancy and obstetric sedation is consistent with two other studies (Brown, Manning, & Grodin, 1972; Zukerman, Nurnberg, Gardiner, Vandiveer, Barrett, & den Breeijen, 1963). Both found a relation between adaptation to pregnancy and analgesic medication during labor. Mothers who are anxious or adapted poorly during pregnancy received more pain-relieving drugs during labor and delivery. The significance of this finding is that a dispositional characteristic of the mother influences a variable during labor and delivery that has clear effects upon the newborn. Thus, a path from the psychological state of the mother, to the behavior of her newborn infant, can be traced with the intervening variable of obstetric medication.

Perhaps more important is the possibility that maternal anxiety during pregnancy may be, in part, reflective of an enduring disposition. Women who are high in anxiety during pregnancy may be those whose general (i.e., nonpregnant) anxiety levels are high. If so, it is possible that the underlying common factor relating pregnancy adaptation, obstetric medication, and postnatal behavior (neonatal through early childhood) is maternal anxiety. Apparent continuity between neonatal drug effects and behavior during early childhood could be a function of maternal behavior toward the infant and child rather than an enduring effect of obstetric medication. Pregnancy to postpartum continuity in maternal attitudes toward the infant has been well demonstrated (Davids & Holden, 1970; Moss & Jones, 1977), as has the early onset of distinctive maternal behavior toward her newborn (Thoman, Lederman, & Olson, 1972). Thus, the only presumption contained in the hypothesis that maternal anxiety is the factor underlying the apparent longevity of drug effects (i.e., Brackbill, 1979a, 1979b) is that the overt expression of maternal anxiety has "negative" effects on the infant and child. This hypothesis, although plausible, remains unsubstantiated.

A more recent study by Standley, Soule, Copans, and Klein (1978) examined an even broader area of potential influences on the infant. Standley et al. obtained not only the standard perinatal variables (labor, medication, etc.), but also assessed the psychological responses (pregnancy orientation) of *both* parents to the pregnancy as well as their age, education, and income. The psychological response of the couple to the pregnancy was assessed in separate interviews with both parents. Interviewers rated the couples' general orientation to the pregnancy based on the couples' marital satisfaction, preparedness for the pregnancy and infant, psychophysiological responses and expectations regarding delivery, and social support for mothers. The perinatal and parental variables were seen as antecedent conditions, describing in a fashion, the earliest environment of the organism (to be born).

Standley et al. found the traditional negative relation between obstetric medication and newborn behavior (specifically, anesthesia and the motor-maturity items on the Neonatal Behavioral Assessment Scale). The authors also found parental age, education, and income to be positively correlated with their psychological response to pregnancy. The parents' psychological response to pregnancy was, in turn, negatively correlated with obstetric medication (anesthesia). Essentially, the higher the socioeconomic status of the parents, the better their orientation toward pregnancy, and the less the obstetric medication (anesthesia) during labor and delivery.

Socioeconomic status continued to exhibit pervasive effects in Standley's data. Socioeconomic status was negatively correlated with obstetric medication and positively correlated with the neonatal motor maturity. Furthermore, socioeconomic status obliterated the relationships between pregnancy orientation, obstetric medication, and newborn behavior. That is, when age, income, and education were partialed out of these relations, all correlations between pregnancy orientation, obstetric medication, and newborn behavior fell below statistical significance. Essentially, a broad descriptive index (socioeconomic status) was exhibiting very focused effects during the prenatal and perinatal periods.

Although the mechanism for the expression of these effects are unknown, some studies (Levy & McGhee, 1975) have suggested that crisis/stress theory (e.g., Janis, 1965) can provide an explanation. As a predictable crisis, parturition is preceded by the information of expectations of difficulty or ease of labor. Levy and McGhee found these expectations to be influenced by the parturient's mother, whose communications with her daughter about childbirth affected the parturient's psychological preparation. Exaggerated communications from the mother, irrespective of the direction of the exaggeration, had negative outcomes on the mother after delivery. Generally, using Janis's crisis theory, Levy and McGhee, and Standley et al., demonstrated that specific expectations of and responses to childbirth were influenced by factors beyond the ken of most studies of the effects of obstetric sedation.

IN CONCLUSION:
THE CONTINUOUS ENVIRONMENT

The data of Standley et al. relating socioeconomic status to perinatal measures has a curious and familiar ring. Socioeconomic status is not a specific variable, but a gross index of many variables, some perhaps too ephemeral to quantify by any psychological metric. Nonetheless, socioeconomic status marks real differences, as psychological research has repeatedly demonstrated. And, if only to again mark the fortunate, socioeconomic status can now add to its list the specific events surrounding parturition.

When considered from the point of view of the maternal-fetal system, one is struck by the "macro-micro" nature of the relation. Levy and McGhee's "crisis" model provides a rationale for perceiving parturition as a focal event, drawing to it the otherwise disparate strands of socioeconomic status. Conceptually, this is close to an approach in family sociology examining life-cycle transitions within the family (e.g., Hill & Rodgers, 1964). Unfortunately, studies within this "developmental" approach have examined the effects of childbirth from the perspective of a normative transition. Thus, the birth process and the newborn infant serve as a "standard stimulus" with pre-post parental responses being the dependent variable (cf., Hobbs, 1965; Hobbs & Cole, 1976). Clearly, a combination of perspectives would be fruitful here. Studies being conducted at the Social and Behavioral Sciences Branch of the National Institute of Child Health and Human Development have taken this combined approach (Pedersen, Anderson, & Cain, 1977; Standley et al., 1978). More needs to be done, particularly in exploring the accumulating number of "curious" relationships between family characteristics and postnatal outcome (for example, *paternal* smoking and infant birth weight and mortality [Yerushalmy, 1971]).

As empirical relations, these are no less puzzling than the effects of maternal social drinking (versus alcoholism) or hormone therapy during pregnancy on infant and childhood behavior (Reinisch, 1977; Reinisch & Karow, 1977; Streissguth, Barr, Martin, & Herman, 1979). The mechanisms by which these various effects might be mediated may be more enigmatic in some cases than others; nevertheless, they all exist.

The hiatus created by the physiological-psychological distinction and the newborn-as-beginning versus end distinction was originated in the service of technological expedience. We still cannot determine the time of conception with any accuracy respectful of the rapidity of zygotic and embryonic development. We remain unsure of the relation between fetal movement and postnatal development (Bernard, 1964; Edwards, 1970; Walters, 1965), much less between prenatal and postnatal learning (Spelt, 1948). We question the viability of hypotheses attributing maternal psychological state during pregnancy to fetal effects transmitted via the placenta (cf. Standley et al., 1978).

But technological expedience rapidly becomes less and less necessary. The early embryonic and fetal environment can be more extensively described today than it could a decade ago. Biochemical assay techniques can detect smaller concentrations of materials in more variegated media. Enhanced image-production methods (fetoscopy, sonography, fiberoptic techniques) yield clearer pictures of the conceptus (e.g., Jouppila, 1975). As amniocentesis becomes safer and as the diagnostic armamentarium increases, its usage will increase, thereby increasing opportunities for normative and descriptive studies.

These opportunities cannot be fully appreciated within traditional disciplinary boundaries. Efforts directed at describing the developmental environment from its origin (conception) onward will require the collaboration of behavioral and biomedical scientists. The large majority of behavioral scientists lack the technology (and technique) required for the *direct* assessment of prenatal factors. The use of measures obtained postnatally as proxies for prenatal assessment are subject to confounding and require, in any case, eventual validation. For example, the use of birth weight (or various weight/length, or weight/gestational age ratios) as an index of fetal nutrition is only reasonable in view of our current inability to assess fetal nutritional status directly. With certainty, this will change in the near future. And hopefully, behavioral scientists will be among the first to avail themselves of those changes.

But what does this say in terms of specific methodological recommendations? In actuality, very little. What is said, I believe, is that behavioral scientists studying early development must be sure to keep a broad lookout for potential influences on their target. In studies of the human neonate, information beyond parity and gravidity should be obtained. The traditional clinical signs (e.g., Apgar, parity, gravidity, labor) may effectively distinguish clinical from subclinical samples, but are probably insufficient to allow distinctions between subclinical samples, or to describe "normal" variability. "Marker" variables are not available for this. Rather, the current zeitgeist should reflect active exploration for potential influence. Maccoby and Jacklin's (1979) recent research involving assays of umbilical blood and motor behavior in early infancy is an example of this type of exploration. Clearly, the work of Waldrop and her colleagues (Waldrop, Bell, McLaughlin, & Halverson, 1978) on the relation between "minor physical anomolies" and social behavior should expand along these lines; these minor anomolies are probably established in the first trimester of pregnancy and may be associated with endocrine function (maternal-fetal) and catecholamine production in particular.

Movement in these directions require biomedical technology. I believe that the most rapid advances will occur among those of us who are able to form interdisciplinary teams with those outside of our field in biomedical areas. The true appreciation of the continuity of early development will not occur until then.

REFERENCES

Bell, R. Q. A reinterpretation of the direction of effects in studies of socialization. *Psychological Review*, 1968, *75*, 81-95.

Bernard, J. Prediction from human fetal measures. *Child Development*, 1964, *35*, 1243-1248.

Brackbill, Y. *Drugs, birth, and children: An overview.* Paper presented at the bienniel meeting of the Society for Research in Child Development, San Francisco, March 1979. (a)

Brackbill, Y. Obstetrical medication study. *Science*, 1979, *205*, 447-448. (b)

Broman, S. H. Obstetrical medication study. *Science*, 1979, *205*, 446.

Brown, W. A., Manning, T., & Grodin, J. The relationship of antenatal and perinatal psychologic variables to the use of drugs in labor. *Psychosomatic Medicine*, 1972, *34*, 119-127.

Conway, E., and Brackbill, Y. Delivery medication and infant outcome: An empirical study. In W. A. Bowes, Jr., Y. Brackbill, E. Conway, & A. Steinschneider. The effects of obstetrical medication on fetus and infant. *Monographs of the Society for Research in Child Development*, 1970, *35* (Serial No. 137).

Davids, A., DeVault, S., & Talmadge, M. Anxiety, pregnancy and childbirth abnormalities. *Journal of Consulting Psychology*, 1961, *25*, 74-77.

Davids, A., & Holden, R. H. Consistency of maternal attitudes and personality from pregnancy to eight months following childbirth. *Developmental Psychology*, 1970, *2*, 364-366.

Edwards, D. D. Fetal movement: Development and time course. *Science*, 1970, 169.

Ferreira, A. J. The pregnant women's emotional attitude and its reflection on the newborn. *American Journal of Orthopsychiatry*, 1960, 30, 553-561.

Hellman, L. M., & Pritchard, J. A. *Williams obstetrics* (14th ed.). New York: Appleton-Century-Crofts, 1971.

Hill, R., & Rodgers, R. H. The developmental approach. In H. T. Christensen (Ed.), *Handbook of marriage and the family*. Chicago: Rand McNally & Co., 1964.

Hobbs, D. F. Parenthood as crisis: A third study. *Journal of Marriage and the Family*, 1965, *27*, 367-372.

Hobbs, D. F., & Cole, S. P. Transition to parenthood: A decade replication. *Journal of Marriage and the Family*, 1976, *38*, 723-731.

Janis, I. L. Psychodynamic aspects of stress tolerance. In S. Z. Klausner (Ed.), *The quest for self-control: Classical philosophies and scientific research*. New York: Free Press, 1965.

Jouppila, P. Diagnosis of fetal movements in early pregnancy. *Acta Obstetrica et Gynecologicia Scandinavia*, 1975, *47*, 53.

Kolata, G. B. Behavioral teratology: Birth defects of the mind. *Science*, 1978, *202*, 732-734.

Kolata, G. B. Scientists attack report that obstetrical medications endanger children. *Science*, 1979, *204*, 391-392.

Kron, R. E., Stein, M., & Goddard, K. E. Newborn sucking behavior affected by obstetric sedation. *Pediatrics*, 1966, *37*, 1012-1016.

Levy, J. M., & McGhee, R. K. Childbirth as crisis: A test of Janis's theory of communication and stress resolution. *Journal of Personality and Social Psychology*, 1975, *31*, 171-179.

Maccoby, E. E., & Jacklin, C. N. *Sex hormones in umbilical cord blood: Their relation to sex, birth order, and behavioral development.* Paper presented at the biennial meeting of the Society for Research in Child Development, San Francisco, March 1979.

McDonald, R. L., Gynther, M. D., & Christakos, A. C. Relations between maternal anxiety and obstetric complications. *Psychosomatic Medicine*, 1963, *25*, 357-363.

Moss, H. A., & Jones, S. J. Relations between maternal attitudes and maternal behavior as a function of social class. In P. H. Leiderman, S. R. Tulkin, & A. Rosenfold (Eds.), *Culture and infancy*. New York: Academic Press, 1977.

Pedersen, F. A., Anderson, B. J., & Cain, R. L. *An approach to understanding linkages between the parent-infant and spouse relationships.* Paper presented at the biennial meeting of the Society for Research in Child Development, New Orleans, April, 1977.

Reinisch, J. M. Prenatal exposure of human foetuses to synthetic progestins and estrogens: Effects on human development. *Archives of Sexual Behavior,* 1977, *6,* 257–288.

Reinisch, J. M., & Karrow, W. G. Prenatal exposure of human foetuses to synthetic progestin and oestrogen affect personality. *Nature,* 1977, *266,* 561–562.

Sears, R., Maccoby, E., & Levin, H. *Patterns of child rearing.* Evanston, Ill.: Harper & Row, 1957.

Schaefer, E. S., & 8ell, R. Q. Development of a parental attitude research instrument. *Child Development,* 1958, *29,* 339–361.

Spelt, D. The conditioning of the human fetus in utero. *Journal of Experimental Psychology,* 1948, *38,* 338–346.

Standley, K., Soule, A. B., Copans, S. A., & Klein, R. P. Multidimensional sources of infant temperament. *Genetic Psychology Monographs,* 1978, *98,* 203–232.

Stechler, G. Newborn attention as affected by medication during labor. *Science,* 1964, *144,* 315–317.

Streissguth, A. P., Barr, H. M., Martin, D. C., & Herman, C. *Effects of maternal alcohol, nicotine, and caffeine use during pregnancy on infant development at 8 months.* Paper presented at the bienniel meeting of the Society for Research in Child Development, San Francisco, March 1979.

Thoman, E. B., Leiderman, H., & Olson, J. P. Neonate–mother interaction during breast-feeding. *Developmental Psychology,* 1972, *6,* 110–118.

Waldrop, M. F., Bell, R. Q., McLaughlin, B., & Halverson, C. F. Newborn minor physical anomolies predict short attention span, peer aggression, and impulsivity at age 3. *Science,* 1978, *199,* 563–564.

Walters, C. E. Prediction of postnatal development from fetal activity. *Child Development,* 1965, *36,* 801–808.

Yang, R. K., Zweig, A. R., Douhitt, T. C., & Federman, E. J. Successive relationships between maternal attitudes during pregnancy, analgesic medication during labor and delivery, and newborn behavior. *Developmental Psychology,* 1976, *12,* 6–14.

Yerushalmy, J. The relationship of parent's smoking to outcome of pregnancy: Implications as to the problem of infering causation from observed effects. *American Journal of Epidemiology,* 1971. *93,* 443–456.

Zukerman, M., Nurnberg, J., Gardiner, S., Vandiveer, J., Barrett, B., & den Breeijen, A. Psychological correlates of somatic complaints in pregnancy and difficulty in childbirth. *Journal of Consulting Psychology,* 1963, *27,* 327–329.

12

Parental Perceptions of Infant Manipulations: Effects on Parents of Inclusion in Our Research

T. Berry Brazelton
Harvard Medical School
and
Children's Hospital Medical Center

PARENTAL PERCEPTIONS OF INFANT MANIPULATIONS

If we are indeed to understand the effects on children of our research strategies as well as the indirect effect on our research results, we must understand what it means to parents to ask them to be included in our research. We must understand the process they go through in consenting to and participating in our request to include them as part of our sample. Or what it will mean to them to refuse to participate. For many participants, consent may be in lieu of saying "no." Particularly, if we ask for their participation around a medical crisis or at a time when they are dependent on professionals, they may not dare to refuse for fear of its effect on their medical care. Their rather magical trust in the medical system and in all of those included in it may cover researchers as well.

Being included in research can easily be seen as an unnecessary manipulation by others. When we ask for consent to include a child in our project, we should be prepared for the question, "Why me? Why my child?" Behind that question lies all of the questioning, the normal concern about the child's condition and/or the parents' concerns about their own adequacy in parenting. A parent must always feel that there is a great deal about him or her that professionals know beyond what he or she is told. If the child is ill, a parent suspects there is more than he or she suspects; if the child is developing normally, a parent questions whether such scrutiny may be based on the researcher's questions about normality. So, the request to join the research cohort takes on added meaning in the light of these questions. The parent–child relationship is inevitably affected by such unconscious questioning. At best, the parent begins to observe the child and the child's behavior much more closely. At worst, the parent questions herself or himself, and begins to mistrust his or her present relationships with the child and with the medical system.

After the initial anxiety and self-questioning, there is likely to be a certain amount of anger and resistance. Recent publicity about genetic research, about manipulative research, all heighten the chances of parents' feeling that the request to be included in a research project is pressure on them beyond their control. Informed consent and our own concerns about malpractice suits often press us to "over-explain" the ingredients and outcome of our research. This excessive information further confuses the parents and they begin to question their wisdom in compliance. They turn to their physicians for advice. Other professionals may sense the anxiety and the questioning behind the parents' requests, and their own natural competition with the researchers may surface. Then, their advice and answers are likely to be even more disturbing to the parents who have consented to participate. As a result, consent on the part of parents is rarely a simple decision. As researchers, we need not and cannot avoid or even allay such feelings in our subjects, but we can expect them, record them and account for them in our results. For they will be influencing the behavior of both the parents and of the child who is our subject. In our own laboratory, filming parents and infants in the face-to-face condition is understandably a stress situation for adults. They are told to behave "normally" and to play with their infant "as they usually do." And yet, we have structured the test situation so that they can touch the baby, but not pick him up. As the parents' own stress in being observed and photographed transmits itself to the baby via their heightened behaviors, the baby will usually indicate that he'd like to be held. *Of course* this increases the violation of both infant and parent expected behavior and *of course* it puts them under more stress in the interaction; but if we account for this in our results, if we describe this as a coping interactional system for the dyad, we learn a great deal about each participant's capacity to deal with stress and respond to the interactive situation *in spite of* the violation. We learn as much about them in this way as we would if we could create an entirely natural situation for their interaction.

If we are asking for participation in a project that concerns new babies, we must place parental responses within the context of their adjustment to their new parenting role with this infant. In order to do this, we must understand the process of adjusting to becoming a parent, of wanting to make it with that particular infant. All parents who *care* (and I believe that all do care) go through an expected kind of turmoil in pregnancy as preparation for their new role. With second and third pregnancies, the degree of turmoil may be different and even decreased, but it will still surface around the questions of sibling relationships, of separating from the older children, of making it with a new, unknown individual.

In the first pregnancy, the turmoil amounts to expressions of anxiety about whether they can become adequate nurturers of the expected infant, and of real ambivalence about whether they even want this infant. The questions of whether they have damaged or will damage the infant are a reflection of deeper ambivalence about themselves as adequate to this forthcoming role. Hence, late pregnancy as well as the perinatal period are periods of heightened anxiety, heightened self-questioning, and heightened ambivalence—about themselves, about the new baby, and, of course, about anyone who intrudes on their new and important relationship. Although their need for support and approval is great, the natural reluctance to share this important adjustment will affect their relationship with observers and researchers.

Even more important, anxiety and ambivalence will heighten their observation and reactions to anything that concerns the new baby. We can expect a powerful Hawthorne (Lana, 1969) effect on the parents' perception of the baby, particularly in the areas we outline for them as our focus. If we are interested in the baby's visual behavior, their anxiety and heightened antennae will focus itself on the infant's visual behavior. They will begin to influence it both consciously and unconsciously. I know that when a mother observes my neonatal exam with me that she will begin to elicit as many of the behavioral responses as she can remember for days and weeks thereafter (Erickson, 1976). Hence, my research exam becomes a powerful model of her future behavior with the infant. To ignore that would be foolish, indeed, if I were looking for controlled results in the areas I have demonstrated in her presence. We find, as a result, that our very presence and behavior as an observer and as an interactant with a new mother–infant dyad become a surprisingly powerful model for increasing interactional behaviors between them, and our research becomes an intervention *automatically*.

By the same token, real or perceived failure on the parents' part as they attempt to model themselves in our image creates even more sense of failure. Parents in our culture do not expect to be successful as parents. Their concern about being the perfect parent leads them to look for failure in themselves and "why me" is likely to be couched in this expectation to fail. They are less likely to believe in their good fortune at producing an optimal research subject for us than they are to feel that we are seeing them and their baby as the failures in our project. The result of this is more sensitivity to any deviance in the infant or to any indication on our part that their baby may not have been the optimal or perfect subject. This reaction is often couched in such tentative but repeated questions as "How did he do?," "Is he all right?," "What do you want us to do?," "Are we doing (exactly) what you want and expect?" Their antennae are out to pick up any slight frown on our face, to ascertain what it is we are looking for, and to press themselves and the baby to produce it. *Of course* this kind of heightened sensitivity will influence our result. The question is not whether we can eliminate such a Rosenthal (1966) effect, for we probably cannot, but how we account for it in our results.

The most serious effect of such parental reactions and concern can be seen in a kind of labeling of the baby, which may go on in parents' minds. In a study of the effects on infant behavior of phototherapy for hyperbilirubinemia, Telzrow and Snyder (1977) in our laboratory found that parents' responses to the depressed behavior of the infants became fixed around the fear of brain damage, which accompanied their awareness that hyperbilirubinemia could, indeed, damage a newborn's brain. The baby's initially depressed behavior after the baby was brought out of the phototherapeutic stiuation was confirmation to them of the infant's damaged condition. In their anxiety and grief over what they perceived as their failure in producing a "normal" infant, they reinforced this initial depressed behavior by leaving the infant alone. They literally placed the baby in a quiet, darkened room in order to protect the baby, feeding the infant only every 4 hours. As a result, the baby's interactional behavior remained depressed for as long as 3 weeks after the therapy. The label created by the combination of the parents' heightened awareness and the infant's initial response to phototherapy prolonged and enhanced the baby's depressed disorganization. None of these infants were indeed damaged, but the parental responses produced behavior that simulated it.

EFFECTS OF OUR RESEARCH ON STAFF

Because a part of a caring physician's relationship is inevitably that he or she wants to guard it, when we include a patient in our research, it sets up normal, natural, and expected feelings of competition in the physicians who are in charge of our subjects. They may respond to these feelings with welcoming open arms, extolling our research efforts to the patients and to the staff. But they may not. They may look for a hidden agenda on our part. They may see our research as a threat to the system, if we are looking at such things as manipulations of the delivery or health care system. If we are investigating the psychological or emotional growth of their patients, they may see us as questioning their own provision of adequate support for the patient. So one can expect heightened awareness of our research and some kind of reaction—positive or negative. Whichever it is, it will be transmitted to the patient and to the nursing staff and both directly and indirectly will affect the very behaviors we are looking at.

Nurses may also feel threatened, but they may want to see change in the directions that our research is leading. They are less likely to be interested in the status quo, and we have found that most nursing staff want to improve the quality of care for their patients. They are usually reinforced by an investigation that leads to change in that direction. In fact, their eagerness to change may be a problem, for there is contamination of controls that they unconsciously produce as their eagerness leads them to change a nursery or to model their handling of the control babies after the experimenters' handling of the experimental subjects. One of the surest ways to avoid this is to gather control data *before* the experimental manipulation is introduced.

There is likely to be a "halo" effect on both parents and child by the eagerness of the nursing staff to cooperate. The interest in the experimental babies and parents expresses itself in increased attention, in increased stimulation, and increased nurturance of both the subject and his or her parents. Hence, a "blind" study in which the nurses or caregiving personnel do not know which subjects are experimental is certainly ideal, but it may be well nigh impossible.

The effects on staff of such variables as SES, single parenting, adolescent mothers, and subcultures are certainly likely to affect their handling of parents. It is less likely to affect their treatment of the baby personally, but I have no question that we create a feeling of "being second rate" in lower SES, unwed, adolescent mothers. And, of course, this will influence their image of themselves as mothers and, in turn, their nurturing of their children. Although there is probably no sure way of eradicating such effects or of modifying the behavior of staff who do not really mean to convey such messages, we certainly must account for them in our conceptual thinking about the influence of such variables and our own compliance with them as we deal with parents who must live with them. A more positive model of looking for and valuing the strengths in parents who must cope with these variables might go farther toward conveying a different kind of message and expectation to them.

In a violated system such as the one we provide presently around labor, delivery, and being in hospital with a new baby, the effects of *any* positive intervention are magnified. Any experience that can be interpreted by the patient as positive or reinforcing for their feeling of self-value or importance to their new infant, becomes of enormous symbolic meaning as they search hungrily for support in such a nonreinforcing system in our present lying-in hospitals. To go on treating deliveries as if they were corrective surgery and patients as if they were ill, insensitive, or both, is patently destructive. Hence, any intervention such as Klaus and Kennell (1976), LeBoyer (1975), or we (see Erickson, 1976) suggest will be likely to produce surprisingly significant results in the light of the mother's (and father's) wish to feel individual, important, and adequate to that baby.

Hence, we must recognize the signal value of our research and its importance in reinforcing parents for their need to feel of value to their babies. Our research becomes an intervention automatically, and as such, parents will utilize all aspects of our contacts in this service. If we drop our eyelids or our voices, parents may interpret that as an ominous indication. If our approval is manifest, they redouble their interest in the baby. Hence, it is foolish to wonder *whether* we are having an effect. A better question becomes "how much and what kind" of effect. Various efforts help us understand our effect—such efforts as controls, blind observers, trained observers for interviewing, setting up our research around a pediatric visit or one that has other meaningfulness to the parents, asking the parents how they see us as affecting their relationship and recording all verbalizations for analysis.

PREDICTIVE MODEL

In longitudinal research, another effort to understand our effect might be accomplished within a predictive model of analysis. By making predictions from one cutoff point to another, and by reanalysis of the predictions for any failure, we can see two things. The correct predictions can be expected if we understand the subjects and their process correctly. Any missed prediction becomes valuable *not only* as a way of understanding the process more clearly, but as a measure of our own bias and our influence on the developmental process. Hence, we can use "missed predictions" to add to our understanding of the influence we are having on the parent–child interaction.

EFFECTS OF OUR RESEARCH
AS AN INTERVENTION

Because we can assume that we will have an effect on the interaction and developmental process that we are studying, we must make every effort to understand that effect. For we can understand intervention better thereby. We can also see our effect on the mother–child relationship as affecting the patients' relationship with medical or societal institution from which we have drawn our sample. Hence, if we understand our effect, we can see how to influence that relationship as well. And intervention or support can be more effectively supported as a result of our research. In this way, as a result of our research we can have a triple effect: (1) directly on the parent–child relationship; (2) by improving the relationship of the parent and the medical system; and (3) by the effect of our research in changing the medical system we are studying.

Our attempts to control and to predict give us insight into the process we are studying. Research gives us insight into the process we are studying. As a result, our respect for parents and their children becomes increased as we understand them. And as our respect increases, our caring for them is touched. Research indeed becomes a way of demonstrating to parents that you care about them and their children—and that's bound to be the most important effect of all on parents' perception of their children!

ACKNOWLEDGMENTS

This work was supported by the Robert Wood Johnson Foundation and William T. Grant Foundation.

REFERENCES

Erickson, M. L. *Assessment and management of developmental changes in children.* St. Louis: C. V. Mosby Company, 1976.

Klaus, M. H., & Kennell, J. H. *Maternal–infant bonding*. St. Louis: C. V. Mosby Company, 1976.

Lana, R. E. Pretest sensitization. In R. Rosenthal & R. L. Rosnow (Eds.), *Artifact in behavioral research*. New York: Academic Press, 1969.

Leboyer, F. *Birth without violence*. New York: Alfred Knopf, 1975.

Rosenthal, R. *Experimenter effects in behavioral research*. New York: Appleton-Century-Crofts, 1966.

Telzrow, R., & Snyder, D. *Effects of phototherapy on neonatal behavior*. Paper presented at the Society for Research in Child Development, New Orleans, April 1977.

13

The Environment of the Newborn in Hospital: The Need to Assume a Patient Focus and a Long-Term Orientation

Evan Charney
Sinai Hospital of Baltimore
and
Johns Hopkins University

There are several concerns that might be expressed about research in the area of care of the newborn infant. First, the problem of an institutional rather than a patient focus to the research, and second, the hazards of taking a short-term rather than a long-term view of the outcomes of care. Obviously, there are numerous other concerns and observations about the nature of clinical research in this area. These specific and selected comments are offered from the vantage point of a clinician who cares for children after they leave the nursery and who is particularly involved in health programs responsible for ongoing or primary care.

Let me illustrate what I mean by the first of these points—the hazard of the institutional viewpoint. Several years ago, at the University of Rochester's Strong Memorial Hospital, some obstetric clinic nurses (in particular the student nurses) became concerned about the environment for patients in that clinic. They noted the impersonal nature of the clinic, the large number of patients herded through the system, the long waits, and the insensitivity of some (not all) of the house-staff physicians and nurses who provided care. In particular, they wished to set up some sort of group counseling program in the waiting area for expectant mothers so that the wait would seem less long and some effective use of the time might be made. Their concerns seemed valid and the suggestions useful. At that time, an anthropologist at the University was conducting a study of about a dozen low-income families in the community, focusing on the use of and attitudes toward health care, among other issues. Her subjects viewed the whole prenatal clinic visit somewhat differently. The entire antepartum visit was seen as a 6-hour process in which the waiting-room time was considered a minor inconvenience, the doctors were seen as well meaning if a bit naive, and the physician visit occupied perhaps 5 minutes of that 6 hours and served a necessary function if you perceived yourself to be sick. Problems that *were* perceived to be important ones included the inconvenience required to get baby sitters for other children (or the decided inconvenience of bringing them along); the bus trip (the route and schedules of which had just changed so that it was not easy to get to the hospital in less than 1½ hours); the occasional nastiness of the parking lot guard who made it difficult to be dropped off in front by car (if a car was available); the downstairs receptionist who checked Medicaid eligibility; the upstairs secretary who determined who was placed in the examining rooms in what order, and so forth. The point here is that although the student nurses were correct in their concerns, their vantage point—the obstetric clinic—limited their views of the larger problem. For the patient, the issues about what made for a convenient and expeditious visit were much broader and probably more significant.

A second episode concerning the same issue of the importance of viewing problems from the patient's viewpoint occurred in Baltimore during this past year. The first marasmic infant I have seen in over a decade was admitted at 4 months of age to our Sinai inpatient unit. The child was born somewhat prematurely to a 16-year-old multipara, and received excellent medical care at one of the area hospital's nurseries. The mother was discharged several days before the child and given a telephone number to call for follow-up care for the child at a city well-child station. A public health nurse made a home visit when the child was 2 weeks of age, having been notified by the hospital of the patient's discharge. It happened to be that nurse's first week on the job and the address she had been given was an incorrect one (the mother had moved); she was unaware of the potential high risk involved in the case and when she was told the patient didn't live there she did not know how to check the neighborhood further to find out where the patient might be located. Her written report to the city noted only that the parent had moved, with no forwarding address given. Finally, when the child was about 4 months of age she was brought in to a health station with a cold. She was at birth weight, marasmic, hypothermic, and almost dead. Why is that case pertinent? Because it reflects a breakdown in the medical-care system, a failure traceable to institutional versus patient-centered thinking and planning. The mother and child had received absolutely first-class medical care in the hospital, the city's health department had a follow-up program, but the two systems had little meaningful communication and interrelationship. Admittedly, this particular parent may not have done well in the best planned system, but the problem was due in part to an institutional orientation; each health unit was limited in its planning and thinking by its organizational constraints, by its own needs rather than being able to fashion a health program based on the patient and family's needs. In research as in health care the central issue is to learn to ask the right question. Certainly those addressing this conference exemplify the ability to ask the right question. The work of John Kennell (in maternal bonding) and Berry Brazelton (in individual differences in newborns) are outstanding examples of the importance of being able to step back from the pressures and routines of presently accepted medical care practices, and to ask penetrating questions about the implications of those practices for the child and family.

The second problem I'd like to identify concerns the hazards of focusing on the short-term outcomes of our health practices. For example, some recently published studies of Robert Chamberlin (e.g., Chamberlin, 1977) are instructive in that regard: Dr. Chamberlin examined the child-rearing styles of parents of 2-year olds, and specifically sought to contrast democratic child-rearing and authoritation child-rearing styles in terms of the immediate and long-term behavioral problems each might produce. The children were first identified at 2 years of age and followed until they entered school. His observations (and others) had suggested that authoritarian styles of child rearing might lead to more conflict in the 2-year-old and then might predispose the child to more difficulties with areas of independence and peer relationships at 5 years of age. In fact, although there were differences evident in the children at 2 years, he could detect no significant differences in functioning of the child and family at 5 years of age. Each group had a similar proportion of behavioral problems. Certainly the multifactoral nature of much of what constitutes the psychological and social areas of behavior make it unlikely that any single factor, be it child-rearing style or presence or absence of effective bonding in the neonatal period, will account for the great variance in behavior seen in later years. We need to acknowledge a good deal of humility in our efforts to explain or predict most of the complex behavior on the basis of any one or two factors, and follow our patients over time.

What suggestions can be made? As health providers we might focus on how we can best provide quality medical care, and, in particular, primary health services to our patients. The neonatologists have done a superb job of regionalizing newborn-care systems, but understandably have been less involved in what happens to the child thereafter. Seeing that our newborns are enrolled in, or bonded to, a primary care system prior to the child's discharge from the hospital must be a high priority. That system should have the capability of outreach and home visiting. Such a system may not have prevented the development of marasmus in the case cited; it would have made it more likely that some team of health professionals know and were known by the family, and might have identified and dealt with their evident problems. What we have found repeatedly in long-term studies is that the environment the child enters after leaving the nursery is a powerful determinant of his mortality, morbidity, and effective functioning. Can we ensure that our patients will be enrolled in a system that will provide the same care and concern over a long period of time as has been provided by those involved in newborn care? I am optimistic that we can devise such systems in this country, and that it will have the capacity to deal with many of the research and care issues raised by members of this group.

REFERENCE

Chamberlin, R. W. Can we identify a group of children at age two who are at high risk for the development of behavior or emotional problems in kindergarten and first grade? *Pediatrics,* 1977, *59,* 971–981.

14 Clinical Nursing Responsibilities for Research Involving Parents and Their Infants

Emmaline Turner
University of Maryland Hospital

In view of the abundance of information acquired through various studies, how is the neonate's environment actually being influenced? What are the responses or conclusions that become a part of hospital routine? What is the role of the parent and nursing staff in effecting change? How can data obtained in studies be generalized to an entire population?

I propose to take a look at these and other questions, strictly from a clinical nursing point of view. One of my greatest concerns regarding research is that little information is filtered to the masses. Whereas the purpose of research is generally to establish a means of effecting change or of substantiating the status quo, those people most closely involved in the care of the neonate—namely the parents and hospital nursing staff—are only minimally aware of the processes or results of research.

Teaching institutions are especially guilty of neglecting the communication of research to those people who actually care for patients. Although research is being carried out daily, it is generally guided by people who do not have patient care as a primary responsibility. Generally, nursing has the greatest contact with patients—more than physicians, and more than social workers or others in the health care team. Nursing in this context is intended to include the professional nurse, RN, the licensed practical nurse, LPN, and the nursing assistant—all of whom come from various educational backgrounds.

Basic nursing programs generally have provided only limited exposure to research design and interpretation. Often the first exposure to research methodology may not occur until a graduate program is undertaken. This limited exposure to research has, in some instances, resulted in a lack of participation due more to a failure in understanding research than to a lack of true interest. Nursing is interested in anything that contributes positively to patient care.

Nursing is in an optimal position to influence maternal and paternal attitudes early in the pregnancy cycle. As the patient enters the health care system for prenatal care, she is usually greeted by a nurse, who performs the initial assessment. With the current trend toward primary nursing as a concept of care, the patient will probably interact with the same nurse on each successive visit.

The basis of care planning and patient education depends on nursing knowledge as influenced by current theory and results of theory testing. *Only* by increased exposure to research and its applications can the nurse be aware of appropriate nursing care practices.

How does the nurse become knowledgeable? How does the nurse perform research on a daily basis as she or he cares for patients? There are two possible ways of doing this. One method is to include research within the curriculums of schools of nursing, thus providing students with first-hand research experience. However, this will affect only one segment of the nursing population. The licensed practical nurse and the nursing assistant would not benefit from such curriculum revisions. Therefore, the employing institution has a responsibility for enlighting these people. Inservice programs can do much to introduce and promote the concepts. However, involving the staff in small-scale studies should markedly influence their attitudes toward research; it is a proven fact that we learn by doing. Also, it follows that such programs will serve to decrease the time lag between the initial recognition and the ultimate implementation of a concept of care.

More information needs to be imparted in a practical way. For example, neonatal rooming-in is encouraged with little or no guidance provided to parents; most mothers have to rely on innate abilities to care for their newborns and observation reveals that many of these caretaking behaviors are in fact inappropriate. There are issues here that pose a major problem for nursing. First, there is the shortage of staff issue (a continual, never-ending problem). Second is separation of staff into distinct categories of nursery nurses, labor and delivery nurses, and postpartum nurses, instead of an interdependent staff focusing on the family unit. Third, there is failure to keep abreast with change. Resolution of these problems needs to be addressed because they pose a major obstacle to the interpretation and reception of research in the area of maternal-child health.

IN CONCLUSION

Attempts to manipulate the neonate's hospital environment will be more successful with involvement of the personnel caring for the family unit. Greater emphasis must be placed on practical, research-yielding information that can be used daily by the staff or parents to foster positive responses such as increased attachment behavior exhibited by parents, increased developmental scores by the infant, or an increase in the quality of nursing care given based on patients' assessed needs.

Generalization of information can only be accomplished by identifying those variables that have broad applications. Age is an excellent variable and parity is another. There are certain predictable behaviors that can be attributed to primiparas, and certain predictable behaviors that are attributable to multiparas.

In summary, a major focus of nursing and research is involvement of the actual caregiver. Researchers must spend some time explaining the problem, design, and interpretation of findings to those individuals most affected. A problem worthy of study can be expected to provide results important to the practice of others. *Only* through dissemination of these results can practice be positively influenced.

V COORDINATED RESEARCH EFFORTS: APPROPRIATE? FEASIBLE?

15

The Importance of Collaboration and Developmental Follow-Up in the Study of Perinatal Risk

Lewis P. Lipsitt
Brown University

We are living in an age of scientific wizardry and rapid biomedical advances. Paralleling the enormous technological strides that have been made in a relatively brief period of time is the speed with which social customs, family structure, communications facilities, and medical care delivery systems have changed. Both of these general facets of modernization—in the intellectual/scientific sphere, and in the area of social mores—have had a deep impact upon the survival of fetuses and newborns, on the conditions under which children are reared and schooled, on life-long medical care, and indeed on conception itself.

On the one hand, it is only a little more than a century ago that one of the first major references appeared in the literature relating prenatal and obstetrical events to the condition of infant survival (Littman, 1979). In his now historic paper, Little (1861) revealed the great importance of any perinatal events leading to neonatal asphyxia in causing neuromuscular handicaps now known as cerebral palsy. In the short period of time since then, of course, this assertion has been verified resoundingly. Much has been learned about the nuances of effects resulting from different types of perinatal risk, including anoxia (Broman, 1979; Broman, Nichols, & Kennedy 1975) and, more generally, about numerous intercorrelated factors constituting developmental hazards (Field, 1979).

On the other hand, it has been only a little more than a century since a virtual revolution occurred in birth styles in the more developed countries. It was then that baby delivery was being moved from the home into hospitals, where only medical personnel and no family members were allowed near the mother during delivery, and where the infant was now considered to be endangered by too close an association even with its mother during the first hours after birth. The gains in survival of babies that have been eventually accomplished through this drastic

135

social change can sometimes cause us to forget that in the early days of this transition the death rates of babies even in outstanding hospitals were actually greater than those for infants born at home (Wertz & Wertz, 1979). Custom changes and intergenerational shifts are very important (Baltes, Reese, & Lipsitt, 1980).

Recently, data have been revealed by Brackbill and Broman (1980) from the National Collaborative Study of Cerebral Palsy, Mental Retardation, and Other Neurological Disorders, which demonstrate some adverse effects upon the physiological and psychological (cognitive) condition of children whose mothers were given certain drugs at the time of the child's delivery. This large-scale study of about 50,000 deliveries, sponsored by the United States Public Health Service at a cost of about 1.5 million dollars, showed that there are apparent deficits in behavioral processes over the first few days and weeks of the baby's life, and also long-term deficits, as a function of maternal drugs. This finding has been met, of course, with much resistance from obstetricians and anesthesiologists. In one report (Alper, 1979), the suggestion has been made that even if the effect found by Broman and Brackbill is true, the finding is no longer relevant, as the data for the study were collected on births from 1959 through 1966. Much has been learned about anesthesias since then, the argument goes, and drugs are administered more conservatively now. Changes in medical customs, and shifts in methods of child delivery, are very important.

Clearly, if medical practice with respect to childbirth can change so drastically in a decade as to render a finding invalid this quickly, it is all the more imperative that we be *constantly* engaged in procedure-monitoring and outcome-assessment programs, so that changes which are made in our understanding of developmental phenomena, and of interventions with respect to child delivery and child care practices will be as well informed as possible.

Closer study must be made, then, of the great diversity of and rapid change in birth practices, the care of the newborn, the conditions under which children survive and grow up, and life-long problems as these relate to perinatal circumstances. It has been amply shown that intergenerational, secular, and historical factors, as well as fortuitous circumstances, do have remarkable impacts on the life conditions and life-outcomes of persons (Baltes, Reese, & Lipsitt, 1980); it is no longer possible for us to assume that when functional relationships are well documented (as between some special parental practice and certain specific child behaviors) this effect will be found one generation later or 100 years later. The multiplicity of events in people's lives conspires to determine life-outcomes, and includes not only hereditary and congenital (endogenous) factors but historical, experiential events as well.

Recent advances in the treatment of premature babies, and other newborns with adverse perinatal histories, have had a considerable effect upon the survival rates of such infants. Small premature infants, who would not have had a chance in two thousand for survival just two decades ago, now survive routinely. Thus there has arisen a greater need for the documentation of the relationship between perinatal conditions and developmental outcomes (Drillien, 1964; Sameroff & Chandler, 1975; Stratton, 1977). Recent findings indicate that prenatal and parturition risk factors may be profitably combined with behavioral assessments of the newborn to identify those whose subsequent development is in jeopardy (Field, 1979).

We now know much more about the ontogeny of the human sensorium, and about the influences of experiences on the young organism, than we did a decade ago (Lipsitt, 1976, 1978; Lodge, 1976). It is the purpose of this chapter, therefore, to: (1) provide a brief overview of our current understanding of the functional capacities of the newborn; (2) suggest that the young infant reciprocates environmental stimulation; (3) indicate that certain identifiable perinatal conditions, some of them a matter of "social custom," place constraints upon normal development; and (4) show that collaborative research efforts relating to perinatal conditions and adverse developmental outcomes have been useful in the past and could become even more valuable in the future.

INFANT CAPABILITIES

The newborn comes into the world with all sensory systems functional. There is convincing evidence that the neonate responds discriminatively to exteroceptive stimulation and that sensory preferences already are present in the first few days of life. Moreover, the neonate may learn to respond differentially based upon sensory preferences and reinforcement contingencies (Lipsitt, 1976, 1979a). Such effects of early experience must have enormous implications for the condition of behavioral reciprocity that characterizes the early interactions of mother and infant (Brazelton, 1973; Klaus & Kennell, 1976). There are reliable individual differences at birth in sensory-motor functioning. Some of these differences can be related to perinatal hazards, such as prematurity and/or small size, the need for oxygen administration at birth, low Apgar scores, or drugs used during delivery (Littman, 1979; Parmelee & Haber, 1973; Prechtl, 1969).

The new expertise in the elaborate assessment of the newborn is certain to have an effect upon our ability to identify heretofore undetected deficits, and to provide intensive follow-up of infants whose development is likely to be hazardous (Field, 1979). Recent technological advances in the study of infants have made it possible to carry out extensive polygraphic assessments of the newborn, which might reveal signs that are not of themselves "deficit conditions," but which perhaps presage a condition of developmental jeopardy yet to be realized (Lipsitt 1979b).

Important advances have been made over the past two decades in the recording and understanding particularly of sensory and learning processes of infants (Lipsitt, 1963, 1976). These have enabled the earlier detection, and often the amelioration, of conditions hazardous to the further development of the child. Health care professionals and researchers with special interests in infant behavioral processes have come increasingly to realize that even newborns are remarkably responsive to stimulation in all sensory modalities. Moreover, the quality and character of the environment play a role in the behavior of the baby right from the start. This means that: (1) behavior is to an extent controlled and modified by the stimulation supplied, either inadvertently or deliberately; and (2) the baby and its caretakers constitute a symbiotic system in which each responds to the other and each serves as stimulant to the other.

The young infant is a reciprocating organism from the outset. Both baby and mother (or whoever is caring for and interacting with the baby) have the capacity to affect each other. Appreciating this goes a long way toward understanding the essence of infancy (and motherhood) and, incidentally, toward appreciating the importance of infancy as practice for the future. By the same token, this view of the infant, even the newborn, as a reciprocating social creature necessitates that we try to understand learning disabilities and other developmental problems in terms of their earliest origins.

Although research indicates that normal human newborns arrive in the world with all of their sensory systems functioning, and even with some specific abilities to learn (Appleton, Clifton, & Goldberg, 1975; Emde & Robinson, 1976; Horowitz, 1969; Kessen, Haith, & Salapatek, 1970; Lipsitt, 1963), there is some controversy concerning "the particulars." There are perceptual and motoric limitations, and newborns cannot learn everything. The newborn's eyes do follow objects; certain colors are discriminated and some are preferred over others. Eye contact with the mother is made by the infant even in the first few days, and the eyes of the newborn function better if the mother has not been heavily drugged at birth (Kessen et al., 1970). The newborn can discriminate the odor of its own mother and chooses to orient more in her direction (Macfarlane, 1975). Taste perception is so acute within the first few days of life that the newborn can discriminate stimulus differences as subtle as 5% versus 10% sucrose solution, and shows preference for the sweeter fluid (Lipsitt, 1976).

Newborns respond with vigorous movements of the head and arms to any stimulus that compromises respiration (Lipsitt, 1971, 1976). The angry avoidance behavior that the newborn manifests when the nostrils are occluded or the head is restrained serves as a hedonic counterpoint to avid sucking and other appetitional behavior, which the infant manifests when presented with pleasant tasting stimulation.

Numerous studies have shown that habituation, or response decrement to the presentation of successive stimuli, occurs within the neonatal period (Reese & Lipsitt, 1970). This capacity for habituation is in fact correlated with such individual difference parameters as amount of trauma incurred at birth. Similarly, cardiac deceleration in response to specific stimulation, representing a rather sophisticated information-processing capacity, occurs predominantly in infants born of conditions that are not generally considered hazardous (i.e., are of normal size for gestational age, are not premature, and do not require unusual care).

The infant's sensory awareness and ability to profit from environmental manipulations has been only recently discovered and emphasized by the professional community. Whereas not long ago there were serious restrictions (see Klaus & Kennell, 1976; Rothschild, 1967) upon the amount of contact that both normal and prematures were allowed to have with other humans (even their parents), this imposed isolation has been lifted noticeably in the past decade. Several studies have demonstrated the facilitative effects upon development of the infant, as well as on the pleasure of parents, of special planned regimens of handling, and interaction (Hasselmeyer, 1964; Klaus & Kennell, 1976; Rice, 1977; Siqueland, 1969; Solkoff, Yaffe, Weintraub, & Blase, 1969). Some of the procedures that have evolved in the infant behavior laboratories already have had practical import. With greater investments in them and in the elaboration of the most promising techniques, further advances can be made in the care, treatment, and even the education of the young child.

Thus the newborn infant is capable of learning. The paradigms yielding the strongest learning effects are those that capitalize upon congenital responses or reflexive behaviors. When positive or approach responses are elicited, such as by stroking the baby's cheek (resulting in ipsilateral head-turning), and the infant is contingently reinforced by the presentation of a satisfying event such as a nipple in the mouth, allowing sucking, those responses will occur more frequently in the future in the same stimulus setting (Reese and Lipsitt, 1970). Aversive conditioning has also been reported in situations where feeding the baby has been accompanied by noxious stimulation, such as undue restraint or respiratory occlusion. This causes the infant to turn from, rather than toward, the feeding situation on subsequent occasions (Gunther, 1961).

MOTHER-INFANT INTERACTION

There have been too few studies conducted to inform us about the crucial early moments of interaction between mother and infant, and about the lingering effects of these experiences. The few studies that do exist (e.g., Gunther, 1961; Korner, 1974; Korner & Thoman, 1970; Thoman, Leiderman, & Olson, 1972) suggest that mother behavior *and* baby behavior are powerfully important in setting the stage for later interactions and perhaps for the discovery of conditions related to developmental aberrations. It is necessary to keep in mind that the mother and infant are a twosome. Each affects the other (Bell, 1971, 1975). Similar observations may be made for interactions between fathers and infants. As little as we know about early mother-infant relations, we know less about the behavioral impact of fathers on their babies, and vice versa.

Experiences in the earliest days of life thus may have an enduring impact (Brimblecombe, Richards, & Roberton, 1978). This has important implications for the facilitation or discouragement of mother–infant contact early in life. Similarly, the extent to which we acknowledge the human neonate to be a fully functioning being with rights to health, welfare, and joy affects our attitudes toward such institutionalized practices as rooming-in and isolation of the newborn in intensive care units.

Technological advances associated with medical care of the newborn have resulted in a marked reduction in neonatal deaths from the beginning of this century (100 deaths per 1000 live births) to the present (10 deaths per 1000). The most recent decade has seen such improvements in the care of high-risk infants, including prematures and small-for-gestational-age babies, that infants who were not viable one decade ago can survive routinely today by means of modern life support systems (Sameroff & Chandler, 1975). The improved survival rate of infants, especially of those with birth anomalies that in previous years would have been lethal, has implications for the survivors. Although prediction of developmental careers from either early congenital disposition or experiential background has never been an exercise of great precision, the changing conditions of reproduction and development in recent years have increased the difficulty of the task immeasurably (Stratton, 1977).

Basic research into the genetic and perinatal antecedents of certain basic psychophysiological processes is a need of great urgency. Of very great potential in the field of child development research is the entire area of mother–infant, and society–infant relationships, in all of their manifestations. The environment implemented for infants is to a large extent a familial and social matter.

DEVELOPMENTAL RISK

There are an increasing number of infants surviving with manifest developmental disabilities, with some of these anomalies, like those of the thalidomide babies, being of immense proportions. Recent perinatology advances have succeeded in reducing the occurrence of certain types of congenital and developmental disorders. It is now possible to assess prenatally certain conditions of fetuses, making it essentially an elective matter as to whether parents will permit themselves to bear, for example, a Down's Syndrome child. The chromosomal anomaly associated with mongolism can be detected through cell examination prior to birth (through amniocentesis), whereupon parents may decide whether or not to carry the infant to term. We need data on the basis of which parents and their professional helpers can make truly informed decisions in such instances.

The precocity of the newborn has implications, not yet extensively explored, for our understanding of the so-called immature nervous system. Now that it is known that the human neonate has all sensory systems functioning and is capable of learning, some earlier assumptions regarding the structure of the early human nervous system must be questioned. Recent evidence from both animals and humans suggests that the period surrounding birth is a time of considerable myelinization, and it is now well established that dendritic development is rapid in the weeks and months immediately following birth. The *process of maturation* may actually be more important than the *achievement of maturation*. That is, experiences occurring in the course of maturation may be those especially responsible for the kind of learning that endures most profoundly. After all, languages seem best learned by young people. Intelligence, moreover, does not change *markedly* after the age of 6 years, and some of the best preserved memories into adulthood and old age are in fact those from early childhood. It could be that the greatest impacts and some of the most protracted consequents of experience are those that occur just when the organism is hormonally and neuromotorically prepared for or ''alert to'' the occasion. There has been some suspicion that this might be especially so in connection with attachment (Emde & Robinson, 1976).

SUDDEN INFANT DEATH:
A DEVELOPMENTAL CRISIS

Great advances have been made recently in the field of perinatal biology and developmental medicine. Numerous developmental aberrations and crises nonetheless remain today almost as much a mystery as they were hundreds of years ago. Crib death, or the sudden infant death syndrome, is one of them. About 8000 babies a year in the United States alone die between 2 and 4 months of age without having manifested any diagnosable problem prior to their deaths. Although some of these infants seem on close examination of perinatal history, or through an incisive autopsy, to have had predisposing deficits, most die of as yet undiscovered causes. There are recent indications, however, that congenital or constitutional factors may conspire with environmental insufficiencies in some cases (Lipsitt, 1971, 1976, 1979b). The following summary of recent data will perhaps show how very important it is to have different institutions, preferably in collaborative communication with one another, working on common problems in this area.

Crib death is the single most common ''cause'' of death in the first year of life, excluding the especially hazardous first few days after birth. The peak incidence is between 2 and 4 months of age, and there is a seasonal variation, with peaks in the winter and spring for the United States. Ninety percent of crib death cases occur before 6 months of age, and 99% before 1 year. Almost every case of sudden infant death syndrome (SIDS) occurs during a sleep period, and the infants are usually found in the morning after no apparent sign of struggle. Babies who succumb to crib death simply stop breathing, at least as far as most later inquiries can determine. There is usually no evidence of any agonal experience, no sign of pain or struggle. Interestingly, and undoubtedly significantly, a mild upper respiratory infection is found in 40–50% of the cases, with the parents reporting a runny nose, raspy breathing, and so on. There is seldom any fever. The baby has been regarded in the few days immediately preceding the death as essentially normal (Valdes-Dapena, 1978).

Explorations into the mechanism and processes of psychophysiological development within the first year of life, coupled with intensive exploration of the effects of perinatal hazards on later development and behavior, including familial and social factors, will probably produce important clues to the causes underlying crib death. It is well known that many congenital reflexes that the newborn manifests gradually undergo a weakening or waning until by 4 to 6 months of age they are no longer present (McGraw, 1943). Some of these, such as the obligatory grasp reflex of the newborn and certain imitative behaviors, are supplanted by more voluntary responses, which ultimately serve some of the same functions as the initial reflex. As cortical innervation progresses, subcortical control of reflexes probably becomes subservient to newly learned responses.

It is a logical and empirical possibility that crib death results either from a premature waning of the respiratory occlusion reflex, or a slow onset in the learning of appropriate defensive responses, which must eventually supplant those disappearing congenital reflexes. The environment may fail in some instances to provide the necessary experiential input to instruct the infant, by the age of 2 to 4 months, in how to defend its respiratory passages against occlusion. Thus experiential factors may conspire with constitutional deficits to create crib death risk.

In one recent study of the developmental histories of crib death (Naeye, Ladis, & Drage, 1976), 125 SIDS victims were compared with matched controls. The data for this study were from the Collaborative Perinatal Project (referred to in the foregoing) of the National Institute of Neurological and Communicative Disorders and Stroke in which 11 cities throughout the nation were represented. The targets of study were all born between 1959 and 1966. The investigators compared the 125 SIDS cases with over 50,000 infants of the Collaborative Study who were born alive and survived the early months of life. This control group was supplemented by another "matched control group" of 375 infants, matched with the victims for place of birth, date of delivery, gestational age, sex, race, and socioeconomic status. All of the matched controls were "survivors." Infants with major congenital anomalies were excluded both in the SIDS and the matched control categories. Clearly, only a major collaborative effort among many research centers could possibly yield such a large sample of cases when the target outcome of interest is of very low probability (2–3 cases per thousand, in this instance).

The study found multiple signs of possible neonatal brain dysfunction in future SIDS victims. Abnormalities were documented in respiration, feeding, temperature regulation, and specific neurologic tests. Apgar scores were significantly lower in the future victims. There was a greater incidence of maternal influenza and cigarette smoking of mother in the histories of infants who succumbed, a finding made also by Bergman and Wiesner (1976). SIDS victims, moreover, had a greater proportion of young mothers of low socioeconomic and educational level, who lived in crowded housing, and had minimal prenatal care. In the Naeye et al. (1976) study, a greater proportion of the SIDS victims were underweight at birth for gestational age. There was little or no suggestion in the histories of any hereditary influence predisposing to crib death. It was noted by Naeye et al. (1976) that many of the crib death victims who grew normally prenatally were growth-retarded following birth, probably not as a result of undernutrition.

In a smaller scale study, again with Collaborative Project data, Lipsitt, Sturner, & Burke (1979) also found perinatal distress related to SIDS. They examined records of the 15 SIDS cases from the Providence population of 4000 births in the Perinatal Project. Any perinatal indices emerging from analysis of such small numbers should suggest predictive parameters for a perinatal risk scale. Such a scale, perhaps with different (or differently weighted) factors in different cultures and regions, would help in the eventual detection of and intervention with infants at greatest risk for SIDS (Protestos, Carpenter, McWeeny, & Emery, 1973). Collaboration among researchers from different regions is necessary for this type of study.

Beginning with the records of the 15 SIDS cases, two control groups were composed, one comprising the next birth into the study of the same sex, and another matched for sex and race. Although there were seven non-Caucasian infants among the 15 SIDS cases, only two of the first control group were black. This corroborated the Naeye et al. (1976) finding that black infants are more likely to succumb to SIDS.

The SIDS group differed from the controls in several ways, all connoting distress or biological hazard. SIDS infants in general apparently begin life with some fragility. The Apgar score, based on a 10-point scale of the viability of the newborn, was lower in the group that became SIDS victims. Neonatal respiratory abnormality was found more frequently, and neonatal intensive care required more often, in the SIDS group. Maternal anemia during pregnancy was present twice as often in the SIDS group than either control. Birth weights and other measures showed SIDS infants to be smaller, and the serum bilirubin levels (related to jaundice) were higher in SIDS than in control infants. Thus, even in a relatively small study, when neonatal risk signs are assessed independently of knowledge of eventual outcome, certain parameters signal the greater likelihood of ultimate jeopardy in some infants than in others.

It should be emphasized that these SIDS cases were essentially normal upon discharge from the delivery hospital, and that they had no overt signs of disease or any alarming symptoms at the time of their deaths. We need to know more about the developmental processes, including environmental factors, that seem to transform minor insufficiencies into such a morbid crisis a few months later.

Previous views of SIDS and its causes have emphasized the prior normality of SIDS victims. SIDS cases appear now, however, to be a "risk population" identifiable in part through their biographies. It is possible that a screening tool consisting of both a perinatal risk scale and neurobehavioral assessment will facilitate identification of those infants in greatest jeopardy (Lipsitt, 1979b). More research is needed on the behavioral correlates or consequences of the constitutional risk factors now associated with SIDS, and on the regional, seasonal, cultural, familial, and historical factors related to this tragic phenomenon. Only collaborative, multidisciplinary, interinstitutional research can possibly develop the full picture.

PERINATAL RISK AND LONGITUDINAL INVESTIGATION

Many studies have been mounted with the intention of discovering the causes of birth defects and residual developmental problems (see Field, 1979). One of the largest scale studies of this type was the National Collaborative Perinatal Project (see Broman et al., 1975). This project, not designed as an intervention study, was descriptive in nature. The intent was simply to record the conditions of prenatal care, birth, and development as carefully as possible, with several institutions collecting comparable obstetrical, pediatric, psychological, and other data surrounding the pregnancy and subsequent development of the child.

There are two major observations to be made about the conduct of that study and its outcome. First, although many "determinants" of birth risk and birth defect were documented to show that neonatal asphyxia is implicated in cerebral palsy and mental retardation and that prematurity is a major risk event in childbirth, socioeconomic level of the parent or parents carried more of the variance (i.e., seemed a more potent antecedent) of developmental outcome (Broman et al., 1975).

The second observation is that although this study was intended to be a descriptive documentation of what happens to pregnancies, and of what kinds of conditions produce what kinds of infants, there can be no question that the conditions of medical practice in the hospitals, and the community care where this study was carried out, were altered as a result of the sheer presence of the study in those environments. If a child were found to have spasticity or an eye defect at the 4-month or 8-month examination, for example, an appropriate referral was made, needless to say, even if the symptoms might otherwise have gone unnoticed. Thus, the study had immediate intervention consequences, whether intended or not. Moreover, the study had direct effects upon medical records-keeping and the quality of medical care in the communities in which the project was carried out. More nursing personnel were hired under the auspices of the project to attend to records-keeping and Apgar scoring in the delivery room, and each project benefited from an influx of other professional and technical help to do the pediatric, psychological and other examinations, and to aid in the conduct of the research generally. (In the Providence cohort of the study, some of the data compiling and records-keeping innovations made for the Collaborative Project are still in effect, and certain follow-up techniques developed under the aegis of the project, such as Bayley testing, are still carried out. The follow-up unit at Brown University still exists, although routine psychological and pediatric examining of the Collaborative Project children ceased in 1972.) Thus the mere presence of a scholarly child development project in a community must be seen as altering the health care standards of that community, even without direct intent.

The latter point is made to suggest that it is virtually impossible in this field to *explore* without *altering*. These verities seem well recognized by contemporary researchers of perinatal risks and their developmental consequences. Future studies in this field must implement research designs that will, first, capitalize upon information regarding known risk factors in pregnancy (e.g., malnutrition, drug-taking, history of pregnancy termination, age of mother) to select a population for study that is, on a probabilistic basis, at high risk for delivery of an infant with defects or developmental problems. The actuarial and statistical technology for this is already available in good supply (see, e.g., Hoebel, Hyvarinen, Okada, & Oh, 1973; Littman, 1979; Littman & Parmelee, 1978; Naeye et al. 1976; Parmelee & Haber, 1973; Prechtl, 1969; Protestos et al., 1973; Robertson, 1979). Second, full recognition must be given to the fact that numerous studies exist to show that birth risk is a function of socioeconomic level, and that socioeconomic level is one of the primary correlates of fetal injury, prematurity, and developmental retardation. Our public health problem requires both improved service to, and intensified research efforts within, the community of parents in greatest jeopardy of having a risk infant. Only in this way will we simultaneously enhance knowledge about the nuances of pregnancy, birth, and developmental-risk effects, *and* improve the sociomedical conditions under which our children are born.

Experimentally manipulated improvements in fetal, birth, and neonatal care, of course, carry some associated hazards with them, both for the child and for the research project. On the one hand, any alteration in the "normal" care and handling of the pregnancy and birth always has some possibility of yielding a deleterious effect. Some of the most well-intentioned, presumably improved, preventative or therapeutic procedures can have unexpected and unwanted effects. Thalidomide, administered at one time to pregnant women as a tranquilizer, produced unfortunate morphological anomalies. Similarly, before today's expertise in the administration of oxygen to asphyxiated infants for resuscitative purposes was developed, dosages were given that are now known to have produced blindness. Advances in care are sometimes hard-won through experimental trials, the outcome of which cannot possibly be known at the outset. This is precisely why, it is argued here, collaborative, multi-institutional, interdisciplinary research *must* be carried out simultaneously with the preventative and therapeutic steps that would otherwise be taken willy-nilly, i.e., without systematic documentation as to their ultimate effects. Only through deliberate selection of a study sample, to whom are delivered systematic care manipulations, which are systematically studied in comparison with systematically selected control conditions, in diverse institutions in a variety of locations, can the appropriate documentations be made that will result ultimately in improved conditions of risk for all sectors of society.

CONCLUDING COMMENT

Documentation of the efficacy of our health care system in relation to pregnancy and childbirth must ultimately be in terms first of the physical and psychophysiological condition of the newborn, and then of the developmental status of the growing child. Various adverse outcomes in the first year of life (e.g., crib death, malnutrition, and failure to thrive) are related to short gestation, small birth size, neonatal respiratory distress, and other risk conditions. These perinatal markers are in turn related to inadequate prenatal care of identifiable and treatable maternal illness during gestation (e.g., diabetes, high blood pressure), and certain environmental and behavioral stresses (e.g., drug-taking, poverty, high anxiety). Data abound, moreover, to indicate that such high-risk conditions tend to compromise the behavioral functioning of the young infant. As a sensing, learning organism, the newborn that appears in the world under these conditions has his or her physical jeopardy compounded by environmental and psychological risks.

Obstetrical and neonatal risk assessments can now be made to enable interinstitutional programs of study through which a protective clinical and research umbrella might be placed over selected infants. The intensity and quality of the child development research effort must match the heroic obstetrical and pediatric procedures that are now technologically feasible. Only then will we approach a full understanding of the mechanisms of fetal development and neonatal survival. We must go beyond that point, however, to better comprehend the perinatal factors associated with the mental (psychophysiological, cognitive, and developmental) well-being of the resulting offspring. The technology is already available to accomplish the task. All that is required is implementation, funding, and inter-professional cooperation. Not to take up the opportunity is worse than oversight.

ACKNOWLEDGMENTS

This manuscript was completed while the author was a Fellow of the Stanford Center for Advanced Study in the Behavioral Sciences, where he benefited from support by the James McKeen Cattell Fund and The Spencer Foundation. Other sources of support, to the Brown University Child Study Center, were The Harris Foundation and the March of Dimes Birth Defects Foundation. Portions of this presentation have previously appeared in *International Journal of Behavioural Development,* 1979, *2,* 23–32, and are reproduced with permission.

REFERENCES

Alper, M. H. Study challenged: Anesthetics given during birth. *San Francisco Chronicle,* October 23, 1979, p. 7.

Appleton, T., Clifton, R., & Goldberg, S. The development of behavioral competence in infancy. In F. D. Horowitz (Ed.), *Review of child development research* (Vol. 4). Chicago: University of Chicago Press, 1975.

Baltes, P. B., Reese, H. W., & Lipsitt, L. P. Life-span developmental psychology. In *Annual review of psychology* (Vol. 31), 1980.

Bell, R. Q. Stimulus control of parent or caretaker behavior by offspring. *Developmental Psychology,* 1971, *4,* 63–72.

Bell, R. Q. A congenital contribution to emotional response in early infancy and the pre-school period. In Ciba Foundation Symposium 33, *Parent–infant interaction.* Amsterdam: Elsevier, 1975.

Bergman, A. B., & Wiesner, L. A. Relationship of passive cigarette-smoking to sudden death syndrome. *Pediatrics,* 1976, *58,* 665–668.

Brackbill, Y., & Broman, S. H. *Obstetric medication and early development.* Presented at meetings of American Association for the Advancement of Science, San Francisco, January 4, 1980.

Brazelton, T. B. *Neonatal behavioral assessment scale.* Philadelphia: William Heinemann Medical Books, Ltd., 1973.

Brimblecombe, F. S. W., Richards, M. P. M., & Roberton, N. R. C. (Eds.). *Separation and special care baby units.* London: Spastics International Publications, 1978.

Broman, S. H. Prenatal anoxia and cognitive development in early childhood. In T. M. Field (Ed.), *Infants at risk: Behavior and development.* New York: Spectrum Publications, 1979.

Broman, S. H., Nichols, P. L., & Kennedy, W. *Preschool IQ.* Hillsdale, N.J.: Lawrence Erlbaum Associates, 1975.

Drillien, C. M. *The growth and development of the prematurely born infant.* Edinburgh: Livingstone, 1964.

Emde, R. N., & Robinson, J. The first two months: Recent research in developmental psychobiology and the changing view of the newborn. In J. Noshpitz & J. Call (Eds.), *Basic handbook of child psychiatry.* New York: Basic Books, 1976.

Field, T. M. (Ed.). *Infants at risk: Behavior and development.* New York: Spectrum Publications, 1979.

Gunther, M. Infant behavior at the breast. In B. Foss (Ed.), *Determinants of infant behavior.* London: Methuen & Co., 1961.

Hasselmeyer, E. G. The premature neonate's response to handling. *American Nurses' Association,* 1964, *11,* 15–24.

Hoebel, C. J., Hyvarinen, M. A., Okada, D. M., & Oh, W. Prenatal and intra-partum high-risk screening. *American Journal of Obstetrics and Gynecology,* 1973, *117,* 1-9.

Horowitz, F. D. Learning, developmental research, and individual differences. In L. P. Lipsitt & H. W. Reese (Eds.), *Advances in child development and behavior* (Vol. 4). New York: Academic Press, 1969.

Kessen, W., Haith, M. M., & Salapatek, P. H. Human infancy: A bibliography and guide. In P. H. Mussen (Eds.), *Carmichael's manual of child psychology.* New York: Wiley, 1970.

Klaus, M., & Kennell, J. *Mother-infant bonding: The impact of early separation or loss on family development.* St. Louis: C. V. Mosby Co., 1976.

Korner, A. The effect of the infant's state, level of arousal, sex, and ontogenetic stage on the caregiver. In M. Lewis & L. A. Rosenblum (Eds.), *The effect of the infant on its caregiver.* New York: Wiley, 1974.

Korner, A. F., & Thoman, E. G. Visual alertness in neonates as evoked by maternal care. *Journal of Experimental Child Psychology,* 1970, *10,* 67-78.

Lipsitt, L. P. Learning in the first year of life. In L. P. Lipsitt & C. C. Spiker (Eds.), *Advances in child development and behavior* (Vol. 1). New York: Academic Press, 1963.

Lipsitt, L. P. *Infant anger: Toward an understanding of the ontogenesis of human aggression.* Paper presented at the Department of Psychiatry, The Center for the Health Sciences, University of California at Los Angeles, March 1971.

Lipsitt, L. P. Developmental psychobiology comes of age: A discussion. In L. P. Lipsitt (Ed.), *Developmental psychobiology: The significance of infancy.* Hillsdale, N.J.: Lawrence Erlbaum Associates, 1976.

Lipsitt, L. P. Perinatal indicators and psychophysiological precursors of crib death. In F. D. Horowitz (Ed.), *Early developmental hazards: Predictors and precautions.* Boulder: Westview Press, 1978.

Lipsitt, L. P. Learning assessments and interventions for the infant at risk. In T. M. Field (Ed.), *Infants at risk: Behavior and development.* New York: Spectrum Publications, 1979. (a)

Lipsitt, L. P. Critical conditions in infancy: A psychological perspective. *American Psychologist,* 1979, *34,* 973-980. (b)

Lipsitt, L. P., Sturner, W. Q., & Burke, P. M. Perinatal correlates of crib death. *Infant Behavior and Development,* 1979, *2,* 325-328.

Little, W. On the influence of abnormal parturition, difficult labors, premature birth, and asphyxia neonatorum, on the mental and physical conditions of the child, especially in relation to deformities. *Transactions of the Obstetrical Society of London,* 1861, *3,* 293.

Littman, B. The relationship of medical events to infant development. In T. M. Field (Ed.), *Infants at risk: Behavior and development.* New York: Spectrum Publications, 1979.

Littman, B., & Parmelee, A. H. Medical correlates of infant development. *Pediatrics,* 1978, **61,** 470-474.

Lodge, A. Determination and prevention of infant brain dysfunction: Sensory and non-sensory aspects. In R. N. Walsh & W. T. Greenough (Eds.), *Environments as therapy for brain dysfunction.* New York: Plenum Press, 1976.

Macfarlane, A. Olfaction in the development of social preferences in the human neonate. In Ciba Foundation Symposium 33, *Parent-Infant Interaction,* Amsterdam: Elsevier, 1975.

McGraw, M. B. *The neuromuscular maturation of the human infant.* New York: Columbia University Press, 1943.

Naeye, R. L., Ladis, B., & Drage, J. S. Sudden infant death syndrome: A prospective study. *American Journal of Diseases of Children,* 1976, *130,* 1207-1210.

Parmelee, A. H., & Haber, A. Who is the "at risk infant?" *Clinical Obstetrics and Gynecology,* 1973, *16,* 376-387.

Prechtl, H. F. R. Neurological findings in newborn infants after pre- and para-natal complications.

In J. H. P. Jonix, H. K. A. Visser, & J. A. Visser Troelstra (Eds.), *Aspects of prematurity and dysmaturity*. Leiden: Stenfert Kroese, 1969.

Protestos, C. D., Carpenter, R. G., McWeeny, P. M., & Emery, J. L. Obstetric and perinatal histories of children who died unexpectedly. *Archives of the Diseases of Childhood*, 1973, *48*, 835–841.

Reese, H. W., & Lipsitt, L. P. *Experimental child psychology*, New York: Academic Press, 1970.

Rice, R. D. Neurophysiological development in premature infants following stimulation. *Developmental Psychology*, 1977, *13*, 69–76.

Robertson, E. G. Prenatal factors contributing to high-risk offspring. In T. M. Field (Ed.), *Infants at Risk: Behavior and development*. New York: Spectrum Publications, 1979.

Rothschild, B. F. Incubator isolation as a possible contributing factor to the high incidence of emotional disturbance among prematurely born persons. *Journal of Genetic Psychology*, 1967, *110*, 298–304.

Sameroff, A. J., & Chandler, M. Reproductive risk and the continuum of caretaking casualty. In F. D. Horowitz (Ed.), *Review of child development research* (Vol. 4). Chicago: University of Chicago Press, 1975.

Siqueland, E. R. Further developments in infant learning. *Proceedings of the 19th International Congress of Psychology*, London, England, 1969.

Solkoff, N., Yaffe, S., Weintraub, C., & Blase, B. Effects of handling on the subsequent development of premature infants. *Developmental Psychology*, 1969, *1*, 765–768.

Stratton, P. M. Criteria for assessing the influence of obstetric circumstances on later development. In T. Chard & M. P. M. Richards (Eds.), *Benefits and hazards of the new obstetrics*. London: Spastics International Medical Publications, 1977.

Thoman, E. B., Leiderman, P. H., & Olson, J. P. Neonate-mother interaction during breast-feeding. *Developmental Psychology*, 1972, *6*, 110–118.

Valdes-Dapena, M. Sudden unexplained infant death, 1970 through 1975: *An evoluation in understanding*. *Pathobiology Annual*, 1977, *12*, 117–145. Rockville, Maryland: U.S. Department of Health, Education, and Welfare, 1978.

Wertz, R. W., & Wertz, D. C. *Lying-In: A history of childbirth in America*. New York: Schocken Books, 1979.

16 Appropriateness and Feasibility of Coordinated Research Efforts

John H. Kennell
Case Western Reserve University

Although every day brings news of another investigator starting a study of maternal attachment, this field is still in its embryonic stages with only limited agreement on the definition of parent-to-infant attachment, its manifestations, and their measurement. Perhaps it is appropriate to turn to the Bible and King Solomon at this point. Working alone and without collaboration, Solomon probably devised the best methodology for measuring maternal attachment. As you may recall, two unmarried women engaged in an old profession had babies 3 days apart. One infant died and its mother took the living baby away from the other mother while she was asleep and replaced it with her dead baby. When the woman woke to find a dead infant in her bosom a great argument ensued, which Solomon arbitrated. He listened to the arguments of the two women, saw that it was difficult to judge maternal attachment by the words and attachment behavior that the mothers demonstrated in front of him, and asked for a sword. He said "Divide the living child in two, and give half to the one and half to the other." One mother said divide it, but the other begged Solomon not to slay the baby; she would rather lose the baby than have anything happen to it. Solomon decided that this was the mother and gave her the infant.

I know there are many creative investigators who will probably be able to devise other measures of attachment and conduct productive research on non-medical manipulations of the newborn's environment, if they have an opportunity to pursue their individual research. I assume that the ultimate objective of the research we are considering is to increase the quality of care of infants and their families. Therefore, I have a heavy bias toward encouraging investigators to conceptualize and test their own individual ideas, whether they conduct individual investigations or participate in coordinated research efforts.

SOCIETAL CHANGE AND RESEARCH PROGRESS

I agree with Richard Bell's emphasis, in his review in *Child Development* (Bell & Hertz, 1976), on the need for research to keep up with, and if possible, precede societal change. In the areas of applied research that we are considering, the dissemination of information to the public is sometimes so rapid that parents have information about the findings before investigators in other centers. On the other hand, societal changes give us opportunities to study the process of change and the effects of the changes. My comments relate to studies in on-going clinical-care situations.

The importance of mother–infant separation during the early postpartum period and the effect on parental attachment would probably not be appreciated if it were not for postpartum separation, which was an almost universal practice in the United States, although clearly *not characteristic* of birth practices in most of the world. Although many centers, in an attempt to keep the family together, have made rapid changes that are far ahead of the knowledge we have gained from research (e.g., having young siblings present at deliveries), the conservative approach of the majority of medical centers has left many other institutions with hospital-care practices that result in degrees of separation ranging from minimal to extreme. These give investigators associated with medical facilities opportunities to study unique aspects of the process of attachment, as for example the work of Susan O'Connor and her colleagues (O'Connor, Sherrod, Sandler, & Vietze, 1978).

The practice of separating mothers and infants after hospital deliveries was established in Guatemala by physicians and nurses from the United States. It has been impressive to us that in one institution almost every time we discuss a variation in hospital practices for the experimental group in a new research investigation, this change has been quickly introduced for all patients. This is in marked contrast to the almost imperceptible changes in most U.S. university medical centers. Perhaps those in such centers can gain hope from an experience in another nation. The second institution in Guatemala appeared to have the medical-center type of conservative resistance to change. Mothers were separated from their babies for the first 24 hours and subsequently saw them only every 4 hours for feedings. Then a major earthquake struck and was followed by after-tremors lasting for 1 or 2 minutes every hour or so for many days. Each one was potentially another catastrophic quake. It was impossible for the nursing staff to take more than 100 mothers and babies outside in this short period so it was necessary to change the hospital policy and to give every mother her baby in bed around the clock so that each individual mother could rush outside the hospital with her baby whenever the building trembled. Other phenomena of nature, such as declining admissions to maternity units, may help us change hospital policies in this country. As a matter of fact, changes in birthing practices and in the manipulations of the newborn's environment are occurring so rapidly in the United States that there are many opportunities for research in clinical units. For example, what were the factors that led to a change? What were the effects of the changes? Of sibling visiting? Of siblings at deliveries? Of the family bed?

Due to the rapidity of change, it is highly desirable that studies of normal mothers and infants occur in institutions with a large population, and that the patients be enrolled over as brief a period as possible. If a study continues over an extended period, it is likely that societal changes will confuse and confound the results. For those carrying out maternal environmental-manipulation research with low-birthweight infants, the small size of the population requires the study to extend over a long period. In our own research this has presented major problems. First, major medical or biologic innovations affecting the care of parents and infants are introduced at a rapid rate. For example, one behavioral study was disrupted because research reports indicated the value of feeding premature babies breast milk. This resulted in a behavioral intervention; that is, a new practice of urging each mother to provide breast milk for her baby was superimposed on the existing study. Other changes in the medical care of mothers (such as fetal monitoring) and of babies (such as transfer to a special care nursery for phototherapy) can have an overriding effect on the behavior of parents and infants.

Of course, there may be an effect in the opposite direction. Our studies of parental attachment in our neonatal intensive care unit have frozen many of the practices and procedures in the unit. Therefore, for 3 or 4 years other behavioral interventions, such as visiting by siblings or grandparents, cannot be introduced. I mention this to point out that only a limited number of studies can be carried out in one nursery. For reasonable progress in behavioral research, it is necessary that investigators in other units be able to study other innovations (e.g., the impact of emphasizing the importance of breastfeeding).

Let me mention a contagious societal change in the subculture of the nursery. Although intense efforts were made to gain the full cooperation of all the staff members in a study carried out in a neonatal intensive care unit over an extended period, we found a leaking of the behavioral intervention to the control group. For example, we found the night nurses in the premature nursery giving infants in the control group part of the intervention designed for just the experimental group. From our experiences in conducting individual as well as coordinated research, we have also found that it is necessary to check and double check what the hospital administrator, the director of a service, or a nursery-staff member may say is the established policy. The investigator needs to see what the actual practice is with his own eyes throughout the 24 hours, 7 days a week. It is a distressing surprise to find that the routine practices are different than what is officially stated, or different than they were at the beginning of the study.

PROBLEMS ARISING FROM
INDIVIDUAL RESEARCH EFFORTS

One lesson I have learned from visiting many special-care nurseries engaged in nonmedical manipulations of the newborn's environment has been to design a study with specific answerable questions in mind. A second consideration has been communication across disciplinary boundaries.

There are interdisciplinary aspects to all research involving patients in health care facilities. With the accelerating rate of change in knowledge and practices, good communication is necessary within an investgator's own profession and across professional lines, as for example from neonatology, to obstetrics, to nursing, to developmental psychology, and back. In the last decade, the large number of studies carried out on the premise that the premature nursery was characterized by sensory deprivation reflected a lack of communication about the noises, flashing lights, IVs, and frequent blood gas determinations that have increasingly characterized these facilities.

Looking back into the distant past, what lessons are there from a collaborative medical investigation that may help us consider the feasibility of coordinated research efforts? My first experience with a collaborative investigation was a study started in 1953 that demonstrated that oxygen toxicity was a cause of retrolental fibroplasia (RLF) in premature infants. I learned three major lessons. First, one had to work on a collaborative project with those investigators who had an open mind or a strong interest in the question being studied. In the RLF study, those with a different conceptual framework did not participate. Second, the primary thrust of the collaborative study was directed at testing the effect of oxygen on the eyes, but in addition the study attempted to evaluate the safety of a low concentration of oxygen. The information gained from this secondary part of the study resulted in: (1) a statement that there was no increase in mortality if the oxygen concentration was limited to 40%; and (2) a recommendation that became a rule—that no more than 40% oxygen concentrations should be used for the care of premature babies. This was the policy nationwide for more than 10 years, but the study had been primarily designed to answer the question about the eyes, not the individual needs for oxygen. Subsequently, it has been shown that this legally restrictive recommendation resulted in the death of many infants who required larger concentrations of oxygen.

In relation to our consideration of coordinated research, the third and most important point I learned from the RLF study was the diversity of environment and care practices in premature nurseries. As similar as two nurseries might appear in all physical dimensions, every nursery had differences, such as different equipment, different medications, and different staffing arrangements. These differences, as well as variation in staff attitude and in the characteristics of the patient population, must be major considerations in any coordinated effort.

From the RLF study, I learned that when a group of investigators from different centers believed that the research issue was of paramount medical importance, they could quickly come to an agreement on definitions such as the description of eye changes; that with adequate financial support, a central research office could be established to supervise the study; that each center could change its practices to conform with the group; and that a common instrument (such as the oxygen analyzer in the RLF study) could be used in each center, provided there was adequate financial support to make the purchase.

It would be unlikely that anyone would contemplate a collaborative behavioral study of nonmedical manipulations of the newborn's environment comparable to the RLF study. It was possible to define the intervention and the outcome measures very precisely—the concentration of environmental oxygen, the presence or absence of eye changes, and whether the baby died or survived.

With a small, well-controlled, well-supervised neonatal intensive care unit or maternity unit, the rapid changes in nursing and medical staff and in medical practices make studies of behavior difficult even with close and meticulous daily attention to the activities within the nursery for both the control and experimental group of subjects. It is difficult to see how this type of supervision could be provided in a study involving more than one unit. The tendency for parents and nurses involved with babies in a control group to make subtle changes as a result of what they see happening to the experimental group, and what they learn from other sources, continues to plague those doing studies in neonatal intensive care units.

Whether or not we decide on a coordinated or an individual investigation, I would like to emphasize the next topic.

PROBLEMS IN DEMOGRAPHIC DESCRIPTION

I would heartily support a coordinated effort to encourage more precise descriptions of samples of parents and children. I agree with Richard Bell that data on characteristics such as race, family income, social class, neighborhood, ethnicity, and language dialect need to be reported. In addition, some description of the institutional and professional attitude and practices is necessary. As David Pederson said, we need to describe the ecology and the social environment of the nursery. From our own research, whether a mother has had contact with her baby in the 1st hour after birth may change the subsequent behavior of the parents and the infant, and this information is usually not obtained and reported.

An effort to work out common definitions, common marker variables, and better reporting of sample characteristics would be desirable, as long as provision is made for flexibility and diversity, with strong encouragement to observe a wide range of outcome variables for parental and infant behavior. It is difficult for individual investigators to achieve what I have recommended for coordinated research efforts.

One positive step would be development of recommendations or guidelines to funding agencies to take a broader view of their research support, to fund a small number of long-term follow-up studies, and to provide support for several investigators to carry out studies on the same population, with travel funds provided for investigators from two or more centers to study the same population group. Support for selected studies for long-term follow-up, long-term funding, increased encouragement for investigators to work in areas that tie in with other investigations, and greater support for instrument development would encourage investigators to work on some of the more difficult questions. Until some of these changes in the direction of research support are clearly stated and these changes are given financial support over several years, individual investigators will still be involved in intense competition for funds, will still recognize the desirability of short-term studies, and will have less incentive to develop common approaches and terminology.

ACKNOWLEDGMENTS

We are grateful for the following sources of support, without which this research would not have been possible: The Research Corporation, The William T. Grant Foundation, Maternal and Child Health Grant No. MC–R–390337-04-0, and National Institute of Health Grant No. NIH 72-C-202.

REFERENCES

Bell, R. Q., & Hertz, T. W. Toward more comparability and generalizability of developmental research. *Child Development,* 1976, *47,* 6–13.

O'Connor, S., Sherrod, K. B., Sandler, H. M., & Vietze, P. M. The effect of extended postpartum contact on problems with parenting: A controlled study of 301 families. *Birth and the Family Journal,* 1978, *5,* 231–234.

VI OVERVIEW AND CONCLUSIONS

17

Comparability and Generalizability of Intervention Research With Mothers and Infants in Hospitals

Richard Q. Bell
University of Virginia

INTRODUCTION

To provide a background for my effort to integrate and discuss the conference papers, I would like to briefly review several particularly relevant points from a paper that I wrote with Tom Hertz (Bell & Hertz, 1976), who was then on the staff of the Social Research Group at George Washington University. The latter is a contract organization that provided research support services at that time for the federal interagency panels on childhood and adolescence. These panels are very interested in any action that would increase comparability of research. Just as in the case of the organizer and supporters of this conference, they are concerned with comparability of research, in the hope that we can speed up the process by which stable, agreed-upon findings emerge. The speed of this process is important because of the rapidity of change in the phenomena of early development that we are studying. For example, in the paper just mentioned, we reviewed one area of research to which social scientists have devoted themselves for over 40 years without producing a body of generally well-accepted findings. I am speaking of the effort to determine the relationship between child-rearing practices and child behavior. At the same time that our research system has been unable to develop a body of solid conclusions, the phenomena of child rearing have themselves changed. Changes over that period have now been well documented, and we face the chilling fact that there is some evidence of societal change that can be detected over a span as short as 2 years (Nesselroade & Baltes, 1974). Turning to examples from this conference, Kathryn Barnard has reported on changes in the nature of infants in intensive care nurseries during the period in which her group has been conducting research.

Furthermore, we need to produce better findings faster in order to justify funds for the comprehensive studies, whose necessity has been pointed out by Marjorie Seashore. Checking on the efforts of possible mediator variables in analysis of the Stanford data, she and her colleagues saw some findings disappear that, without such controls, would have been accepted and published. Their analysis of the data strongly pointed to the need for multivariate analyses. As we all know, these require much larger samples than most of us have been able to attain. Larger samples require better research support.

One other consideration in speeding up the process of producing dependable findings involves the use of marker variables. In my paper with Hertz, I mentioned that a large number of studies on Headstart could not be used in Bronfenbrenner's (1975) review because they had not used comparable instruments to assess development. This same problem has been pointed out in Allen Gottfried's review of the literature (Cornell & Gottfried, 1976) on studies of prematures that he summarized at this conference. The use of marker variables is one means of increasing the comparability of research. Other means involve small-scale collaborative efforts, and better reporting of the nature of samples and procedures.

Generally speaking, in intervention research, we are not directly seeking what has been called by Weisz (1978) *transcontextual* findings. Examples of transcontextual findings have been pointed out in my paper with Hertz. We cite the broad applicability of learning principles that were actually derived from pigeons and rats. Another example is the invariance of the stages of sensori-motor development across social classes, and even between man and other mammals. For example, the stages have even been shown to exist in Rhesus monkeys.

Transcontextual principles may result from intervention research, although these are not direct objectives. For example, in order to explain findings involving intervention in early infancy, Hunt (1966) formulated what he called the "problem of the match." This broadly applicable principle states, in effect, that every intervention changes the nature of our target. If we are successful in getting an infant to develop expectancies relative to the environment, then we have an infant for whom our previous intervention is less applicable, and who requires a new kind of intervention. That is, we have a moving system. One other example is Skeels' (1966) findings on the intellectual development of 17-month-olds transferred from an orphanage to the care of young retarded women in another institution. These findings have gradually led to a complete revision of our views on the importance of early development, but they were the result of a fairly simple intervention strategy. Such powerful, highly generalizable findings are an occasional byproduct but not a direct result of the applied research objective we pursue in intervention research. It is in such research that we customarily see a large number of studies carried out before we can estimate the gist of the findings for an area. In this kind of research there is good reason to be concerned about comparability of research, and any means of accelerating the process of reaching generally acceptable findings is important. On the other hand, concerns about comparability of research are not appropriate at the cutting edge of science, where very novel studies and new leads are being pursued for the first time. In such areas, concerns about comparability would be stultifying and inappropriate.

COLLABORATIVE RESEARCH

There was little dissent made from two points during the conference, which, considered together, point toward a need for collaborative research. I have already mentioned that Marjorie Seashore sees in the analysis of the Stanford studies an argument for larger as well as more heterogeneous samples. Kathryn Barnard has also pointed up the need for longer follow-ups. Small-scale, flexible, collaborative projects could make it possible to achieve both objectives simultaneously. For example, the collaboration of only three projects, whose investigators have reported findings at this conference, would make possible substantially larger and more heterogeneous samples, some from very different social, economic, and ethnic groups. Collaboration would also make possible more sustained follow-ups. Although peer review groups ultimately determine whether research proposals are funded, including collaborative studies such as I am suggesting, all federal agencies that provide money to support child development research have now been sensitized to the need for such collaboration.

Obviously, much more planning and cooperation would be necessary in preparing a proposal for collaborative research. The groundwork could be laid by meetings of potential collaborators at scientific conventions; support could then be requested for the efforts that were already underway on an informal basis. Examples of small-scale, flexible collaborative projects have been provided in my paper with Hertz. I can add another example from the work of investigators participating in this conference. Berry Brazelton, in developing his neonatal assessment scale (1973), worked very effectively with investigators at several different sites in this country.

Most of the conference participants are familiar with the difficulties in applying for and obtaining funding for research: the amount of time necessary to prepare an application; defense of the proposal before peer review committees and site visitors; and, after success in this phase, the difficulties of managing a single project so that it runs smoothly and yields an optimal return. Furthermore, most investigators have experienced the coercive effect of their own research plans. That is, once one has said what will be done, it is necessary to carry out the study in order to fulfill the agreement with the granting institution. Occasionally, one's own proposal can seem like a straightjacket when developments occur that would suggest deviations from the original plan. In the face of the foregoing, what kind of lunacy does it require to contemplate a collaborative project?

First of all, relative to the straightjacket, a collaborative project can offer more freedom than one might expect. Only the core research program need be carried out by all investigators. Ancillary projects that extend and complement the core project may differ among collaborators. In fact, it is worth noting that the tremendous upsurge of research in infancy that developed in the 1960s was a result of *ancillary* projects being carried out by each one of the collaborating institutions, rather than as a result of the core project common to all in the gigantic research program of the National Institute of Neurological Diseases and Stroke (NINDS) that involved 12 institutions and 44,000 subjects (Broman, Nichols, & Kennedy, 1975).

In addition to teaching us the wisdom of carrying out small-scale rather than large collaborative efforts, the NINDS project has shown us the need for much more planning time, much more time for pilot studies, and the need for training and calibration of testers and observers. Does this seem as though it is "pie in the sky?" Fortunately, there is a recent example of a major governmental agency providing for a 1-year planning period in setting up research organizations. The Bureau of Education for the Handicapped, Office of Education, established five institutes for research on learning disability in the fall of 1977, and provided each with 1 year for planning.

SINGLE SUBJECT DESIGNS

The need for pilot studies brings up the possible role of intensive studies of individual cases. Here also I see many indications of the value of a particular research approach in meeting needs that have been expressed by conference participants. One implication of many comments made at this conference is that we should have detailed and comprehensive studies of the kind that can be carried out more readily with individuals or a small number of cases. Examples are David Pederson's, Evan Charney's, and Berry Brazelton's pleas for a better description of the social and physical environment, and for anthropological studies of pregnancy; Lewis Lipsitt's arguments for the importance of studying intermediary processes; and Kathryn Barnard's filming of what is actually going on in caregiving operations in a nursery. Basically, it appears to me that all these comments add up to the fact that we need to know what is going on in a system before we undertake intervention.

Not only do we need more pilot studies to find out in detail what is going on, we need to simply take cognizance of facts that are already in the literature. We should be cognizant of known salient features of the infant-caregiver system during the period in which our interventions are planned. Fortunately, Emde, Gaensbauer, and Harmon (1976) have provided a comprehensive review of changes in infant capabilities and maternal reactions during the first 2 years. Taking into consideration the infant's sleep and waking patterns, as well as capabilities for transactions with the environment, they have built up a very intriguing case for a period of reorganization at the 2nd and 7th months of development. In my book with Harper (Bell & Harper, 1977, Chapter 6), I have extended these points on transition periods and changes in infant behaviors into a set of hypotheses concerning the effects of the infant on the caregiver during each of these periods. We can expect that these efforts to collate and synthesize available information on salient features of the early infant-caregiver system will be modified and amplified as results from further studies come in. Current interests that may lead to modification are Mary Anne Trause's hypothesis concerning en face as an attachment mechanism, and Berry Brazelton's reports of gaze aversion developing during the 12-week period.

The foregoing considerations point to the need for fine-grain studies of the infant-caregiver system and its context, and a better cognizance of the existing literature on salient features of development. Whether as a prelude to a collaborative effort, or as a simple effort to lay the groundwork for an individual research project, it seems highly desirable that pilot studies be carried out with small numbers of case studies before launching a major intervention effort. The next question is whether one follows up such efforts by proceeding to a formal research design in which experimental and control groups are contrasted. The answer is, "not necessarily." Our colleagues in the field of education, psychology, and psychiatry, who are interested in applying behavior modification techniques to a wide range of human problems, would say that we should first employ single-subject designs to see whether the planned intervention can be seen to work in the individual subject before setting up a group design. They might also point out that single-subject designs may also be embedded in group designs so that one knows on the level of the individual case what is going on to produce the effects in the group.

If we followed Skinner's dictates, we would not consider that we have achieved control of behavior unless our intervention can cause it to shift from its baseline and return when the intervention is terminated. Thus, many investigators would not undertake single-subject research studies in which the intervention could be expected to produce an irreversible change. Also, for ethical reasons, we may not want to reverse an improvement that we have produced. However, there are other single-subject designs that do not depend on reversibility—multiple baseline, multiple schedule, and concurrent schedule (Hersen & Barlow, 1976). Thus, there are very few phenomena for which it would not be possible to carry out a planned intervention in which individual subjects are observed intensively. In this way, we can see whether we are getting the planned effect in the individual case, reversible or not, before proceeding to a formal design.

In any event, in order to exercise responsibility in the use of taxpayers' funds for research, we would want to assure ourselves that we have good grounds for expecting a formal research project with a large number of cases in its contrast groups to work, before we expend the public funds that are required for such a project.

For those who are in agreement with this line of thought relative to research approach, the next question might be that of adjusting single-subject designs in an intervention study to the successively emerging characteristics of the infant-caregiver system. For the changing nature of the mother's psychology in pregnancy, the changes in the mother–infant system in the hospital, and in the remainder of the 1st year, it appears quite unlikely that an intervention that is appropriate for one phase would be appropriate for another. The initial and repeated interventions need to be adjusted to the salient features of the system at the points of intervention. With at least one notable exception, yet to be replicated consistently (Klaus & Kennell, 1976), it does not appear that an initial intervention could serve as an innoculation. Even if the model of immunization were appropriate, we would still expect that booster shots would be needed.

If intervention research on manipulation of the neonate's hospital environment follows the general trend of results from other intervention research (such as the many studies of infancy and the early preschool period in connection with Headstart), it is most likely that *sequences of intervention,* each adapted to the demands or tasks of the infant-caregiver system during particular phases, will show the greatest long-term effects. Michael Yogman pointed out an unusually effective use of a salient feature of development: Klaus and Kennell provided an opportunity for mother–infant interaction at the time that visual alertness is so prominent in the infant, 2 to 3 hours postpartum. The eye-to-eye contact of mother and infant apparently played a very important role in bonding the pair. He also mentioned another phenomenon that would affect the efficacy of intervention, the infant's gaze-aversion at around 12 weeks. The data of Emde et al. (1976) would indicate that an intervention in the period before 8 weeks would encounter a fundamentally different infant-caregiver system than that existing after this period. It should also be kept in mind that an intervention at Time 2 would have to be adjusted to the changed status of the subject resulting from intervention at Time 1, even if there had been no marked general developmental change between the two time periods. I have already mentioned that this is what Hunt refers to as "the problem of the match."

In Anneliese Korner's study of apneic episodes, we have an example of what might have happened had one employed single-subject designs in a pilot study. From her data, it appears that only one out of eight individual subjects would have yielded misleading data relative to the eventual group results. Obviously, by chance one might unfortunately encounter a series of cases at the very beginning of a study that produced results running in the opposite direction, or one might have the kind of finding that can only be demonstrated in terms of small differences in large samples. If such things didn't happen, there wouldn't be any need for sampling theory in statistics. Even in such cases, however, it might be very informative to study intensively cases that are not yielding results in the expected direction. The data from such cases might make it possible to review the theory involved, and provide a better focus for the main study. It might also be possible to sharpen the objectives of the study, and control some variables that produce the unexpected performance in the pilot studies, so that such large numbers of subjects would not be necessary to support conclusions in the final study.

SAMPLING FROM THE
BIOLOGICAL-EXPERIENTIAL RISK MANIFOLD

There are several straws in the wind indicating that it would be productive to use a combination of biological and experiential risk factors in selecting neonates for intervention in hospital settings. Sameroff (1975) has noted that the interaction of prematurity and social class status resulted in a much greater effect on the developmental status of subjects in long-term follow-ups than did either factor by itself. Premature infants from lower income homes showed deficits on the order of 19–37 IQ points, in contrast to much smaller and almost socially insignificant deficits (5-7 points) associated with prematurity as such. Informal reports reaching me from Arthur Parmelee's study of risk infants at UCLA indicate that the combination of biological and social risks was again a much more powerful source of determination than either one by itself. The Foundation Fund for Psychiatry has shifted its support toward studies of schizophrenia that test the interaction of the biological and experiential risk factors in that disorder as well. In short, there are studies from other areas of research, as well as those involving manipulation of the neonate's hospital environment that indicate paydirt may be in the interactions rather than in the main effects.

SAMPLE DESCRIPTION

Even if collaborative efforts might not be feasible, considerable gain in comparability may result simply from better specification of how samples have been selected, and from a more complete description of independent and dependent variables used. Put yourself in the position of a reviewer who is sifting through all of our studies 10 years from now. The reviewer may have been commissioned by some foundation or governmental agency, and asked to state what has been learned from the last 10 years of research involving manipulation of the neonate's hospital environment. Now imagine that there are results from some studies that do not agree with those from others. The first thing the reviewer will look at is the nature of the samples. If the description of the sample includes age, sex, social class, ethnic origin, and other vital information, as well as the means by which the sample was obtained, it might be possible to unscramble the discrepancy. It was by such a process that Bronfenbrenner (1975) discovered that

Headstart projects reporting large differences between experimental and control groups, in contrast with those reporting small differences, had permitted experimental groups to select themselves for the program, and thus had obtained an unusually motivated group that was not comparable to the control groups.

Journal editors make it difficult to report fully and completely on the nature of one's sample, and they restrict the description of measures used because of the cost of journal space. However, it is possible for the investigator to file more complete reports with documentation services, and in the case of large-scale expensive intervention projects, it is a service to one's colleagues to maintain complete descriptions of the sample and instruments available for at least 10 years after termination.

One of the problems in sample selection is that the number of cases needed increases dramatically as a function of the number of variables in the selection process. For example, assuming we have reached the point of doing a study involving group contrasts. With 2 variables measured dichotomously we have 4 cells, and thus would need 8 cases simply to have *any* within-cell variance to use in an error term. Although it is desirable to *record* data on as many sample characteristics as possible, it is certainly not desirable to *select* on the basis of any more variables than those that are clearly relevant. From the Stanford data, it is clear that parity is one such variable for most studies in our area of research.

What happens next if one still has a large number of such variables that need to be considered in sample selection, even after giving each a critical evaluation on the basis of relationships reported in past studies? One possibility is to develop a risk composite. This is the approach that has been used by Arthur Parmelee (Parmelee & Haber, 1973). It is necessary to first establish the nature of the interrelations between these variables before one develops a composite. Otherwise, one might be adding components together that operate negatively rather than positively. Discriminant function analysis provides a sophisticated method of weighting a set of variables used in a selection process, but one must use a very large sample relative to the number of variables, or the weighting scheme will be unreplicable.

Given a small number of variables, or a composite that can be used as the basis for sample selection, one could again profitably consider whether it would be well to select individual subjects for intensive pilot studies from each of the cells in the sampling manifold, or from points on the distribution of the composite. Again, Evan Charney has presented the case for focusing on the details of the process in individual cases. There is another reason why this prior approach to formal research designs may be of considerable merit. One should consider that a formal research project involving a contrast of large groups may yield a negative result that is in error, and such a negative result, as well as the reasons for it, could well emerge from an intensive study of the individual subjects undertaken before launching the formal design.

MARKER VARIABLES AND COMPARABILITY

One reason research on early stimulation of rodents progressed so rapidly in the 1960s was that almost all studies employed the open field test at the same phase of the animals' development, and derived almost the same measures. By way of contrast, it took the efforts of several reviewers and a delay of many years before it was possible to derive some conclusions from the Headstart studies, because only a small number of these many studies used the same measuring instruments. Whereas those who carried out the studies of rodents placed a high value on alignment and comparison of their results with those of previous studies, many of the investigators in Headstart programs selected tests on the basis of their own personal preferences. We also know that in many areas of research on human subjects there is a tendency to be as creative as possible, to come forth with new ways of measuring things, to constantly refine or improve instruments used in the past. There are good reasons for this. Progress in our field depends in part on innovation in measurement. Research could very well become stultified if investigators continued research with the same measures year after year. As Kathryn Barnard has pointed out, the measures used depend on the development of the field, and we have heard some suggestions for new measures. Mary Anne Trause suggested that we might try Robson's (1967) and Stern's (1974) measures of eye-to-eye contact. Allen Gottfried has pointed to the value of studying cross-modal transfer in order to get at the development of integration.

By itself, the constant development of new instruments poses no problem for comparability. The problem lies not in the new instruments that are used, but in the failure to include in the project the standard instruments that are used by most others in this same area of research. One cannot count on these standard and most frequently used instruments as being the most sensitive to detect effects, but inclusion of one or more may be critical relative to comparability and generalizability within the field of research. It is not necessary to use a large number of such marker measures, but rather, only those that have been used in most studies in the area with which one's own research can be compared, and then only those that have shown some relationship to outcomes of intervention. The Brazelton can be used during the newborn period. Howard Moss' (1967) and Leila Beckwith's (1972) home observation system can be used for the 1st through the 3rd month. Mary Ainsworth's (Ainsworth & Bell, 1970) strange situation test can be used toward the end of the 1st year. If such measures are used for marker purposes, they should be used exactly as they have been used in most previous studies or, if there has been variation from study to study, as in the most critical studies with which one's own results are going to be compared. Even if only one other study has been done in a particular area in which one is interested, there will be general benefit to the field from repeating one measure that was found to be related to the dependent or outcome variable. There would be some gain in including such a measure even if it were only used in a pretest or post-test assessment.

The result is that inclusion of measures for marker purposes need not restrict the investigator's innovation in measurement, and will make it more likely that an effort at synthesis several years hence will be more successful. It is also possible that the data from the marker measure will make it possible to include a study with several others that will contribute to theory or that will guide policy, whereas a project may be simply recorded without recognition of its findings, if there is no basis for including it with others. So far, in most areas of intervention research, no single study has been critical, although many individual studies have provided considerable excitement and interest. Results that seem sufficiently well-agreed-upon to guide further research and public policy have been gleaned from many projects conducted over many years.

GENERAL PROBLEMS IN
INTERVENTION RESEARCH

One problem of intervention research mentioned in this conference is the fact that any innovation is attractive to nursing and other staff, making it difficult not to use the program with a control group. In the present area of research, I haven't seen any use of what is called a "first wave control." This is a control group studied before the intervention program is launched. Possibly the "first wave control" has not been used because of concerns about seasonal or periodic variations in the nature of the mothers and infants being served by a hospital. Thus, a control group for whom one obtains pre- and post-measures may not be comparable with an experimental group that follows. However, it seems to me that, in most cases, such a control group could be selected so as to be comparable. At least, the question of whether it was comparable can be evaluated empirically. As soon as the second or experimental wave of subjects is processed, it can be determined rather quickly, on the basis of pretest measures, whether one has comparable groups. Of course, it is possible to match cases from the second wave of subjects with those already obtained for the first wave.

One other problem concerns relationships to the mass media. Early in this paper, I mentioned that the problem of rapid change in our society is an important reason for accelerating the process by which our research establishment attains findings for which there is some consensus among scientists. We need to derive conclusions at least more rapidly than the changing societal structures to which they apply. We can't do anything about the profound population and technological changes that are producing so much instability in our society, but we can have an effect on another source of societal change that results from our own efforts. Time and time again social behavioral, and medical scientists have announced exciting new findings coming from their research, aroused the public, which has attempted to adjust to the implications of the findings, only to find out a few years later that other investigators could not replicate the results, or that an artifact produced the originally exciting findings. We certainly don't want to set ourselves apart from society as an Egyptian priesthood in which information is kept from the public because it is assumed that they wouldn't know how to use it. On the other hand, it seems to me that the communication of research to the mass media should be at the point when some general findings have emerged from several years of research, and when there is agreement among most investigators about the nature of these findings. We have an increasingly well-educated population that wishes to use research information to guide their lives. They have a capability of benefiting from all the useful information that comes out of public and private support of science. However, if we report isolated findings that have not yet been substantiated by others, we run the risk ourselves of contributing unnecessarily to societal change. The vacillations in policy toward child-rearing practices expressed in successive editions of government pamphlets on child care, to which my paper with Hertz has referred, provide abundant evidence that the research establishment has contributed to societal instability. Most of the major shifts that occurred in the government pamphlets were based on the enthusiasm and personal convictions of scientists who were called in as experts. They were not based on solid, dependable facts.

Restraint is clearly in order. The fact that a reporter finds something of interest in one's research and wishes to make a story out of it is not by itself an adequate basis for communicating the finding to the public. Of course, all of us are under pressure from institutions to publicize research, even ongoing research, to bring credit to the institution and support from Congress and legislatures. Considering that in many cases an investigator must yield in some way to this pressure, I'm always pleased when I see in a report for the mass media, clear statements that the finding is tentative, needs much further study, and affords no basis for a change in present practices. There is an additional reason for minimizing communications to the mass media until clear and obvious patterns of findings have emerged from many investigations. The effects of the mass media can be so dramatic that one's own research is impaired. Although we are still trying to determine the effects of early stimulation on infants, mothers are already attaching bulls-eye and checkerboard patterns to the sides of infant's cribs.

SUMMARY

Intervention in the neonate's hospital environment is experiencing problems similar to those in other areas of intervention. Because of the way we carry out our social, behavioral, and medical research, findings from different studies are often difficult to compare, and the rate at which we generate dependable conclusions may not be sufficient to stay ahead of societal changes affecting mothers and infants in hospitals. Because the results from individual studies are unlikely to be decisive, and most often we are seeking a pattern of results that can be seen across many investigations, small scale, flexible, collaborative research may accelerate the process of reaching firm conclusions. Collaboration on the core program would make it possible to study larger samples over longer time periods, whereas variations from project to project in ancillary research could provide the freedom for individual variation that is also so necessary for research progress. Collaborative efforts require a longer preparation time, so pilot studies and single-subject designs are advocated as a means of previewing the complex bio-social systems that we study, as well as the metamorphic changes within these systems. Where collaboration is not feasible, complete sample description and the use of marker variables can assist generalizability between studies. Selection of individuals for intensive studies should, if possible, be on the basis of both biological and experiential risk factors, because recent research indicates that the interaction of both factors makes a much more powerful contribution to development than either by itself. Other problems discussed are premature attitude changes in staff that make it difficult to provide control groups for an experimental intervention, and the problem of communicating research results that may produce unnecessary oscillations in public attitudes and practices, as well as adversely affect ongoing research.

REFERENCES

Ainsworth, M. D. S., & Bell, S. M. Attachment, exploration, and separation: Illustrated by the behavior of one-year-olds in a strange situation. *Child Development,* 1970, *41,* 49–67.

Beckwith, L. Relationship between infants' social behavior and their mothers' behavior. *Child Development,* 1972, *43,* 397–411.

Bell, R. Q., & Harper, L. V. *Child effects on adults.* Hillsdale, N.J.: Lawrence Erlbaum Associates, 1977.

Bell, R. Q., & Hertz, T. W. Toward more comparability and generalizability of developmental research. *Child Development,* 1976, *47,* 6–13.

Brazelton, T. B. Neonatal behavioral assessment scale. *Clinics in Developmental Medicine,* (No. 50). Philadelphia: J. P. Lippincott, 1973.

Bronfenbrenner, U. Is early intervention effective? In B. Z. Friedlander, G. M. Sterritt, & G. E. Kirk (Eds.), *Exceptional infants: Assessment and intervention.* New York: Brunner/Mazel, 1975.

Broman, S. H., Nichols, C. L., & Kennedy, W. A. *Preschool IQ: Prenatal and early developmental correlates.* Hillsdale, N.J.: Lawrence Erlbaum Associates, 1975.

Cornell, E. H., & Gottfried, A. W. Intervention with premature infants. *Child Development,* 1976, *47,* 32–39.

Emde, R. N., Gaensbauer, T. J., & Harmon, R. J. Emotional expression in infancy: A biobehavioral study. *Psychological Issues* (Monograph Series), 1976, *10* (1, Serial No. 37.).

Hersen, M., & Barlow, D. H. *Single case experimental designs: Strategies for studying behavioral change.* New York: Pergamon, 1976.

Hunt, J. McV. Toward a theory of guided learning in development. In R. H. Ojemann & K. Pritchett (Eds.), *Giving emphasis to guided learning.* Cleveland, Ohio: Education Research Council, 1966.

Klaus, M. H. & Kennell, J. H. *Maternal–infant bonding*. St. Louis: Mosby, 1976.

Moss, H. A. Sex, age, and state as determinants of mother–infant interaction. *Merrill-Palmer Quarterly*, 1967, *13*, 19–36.

Nesselroade, J. R., & Baltes, G. B. Adolescent personality development and historical change: 1970–72. *Monographs of the Society for Research in Child Development*, 1974, *39* (Serial No. 154).

Parmelee, A. H., & Haber, A. Who is the risk infant? In H. J. Osofsky (Ed.), *Clinical obstetrics and gynecology*. New York: Harper & Row, 1973.

Robson, K. S. The role of eye-to-eye contact in maternal–infant attachment. *Journal of Child Psychology and Psychiatry*, 1967, *8*, 13–25.

Sameroff, A. J. Early influences on development: Fact or fancy? *Merrill-Palmer Quarterly of Behavior and Development*, 1975, *21*, 267–294.

Skeels, H. M. Adult status of children from contrasting early life experiences. *Monographs of the Society for Research in Child Development*, 1966, *31* (Serial No. 105).

Stern, D. N. Mother and infant at play: The dyadic interaction involving facial, vocal, and gaze behaviors. In M. Lewis & L. A. Rosenblum (Eds.), *The effect of the infant on its caregiver*. New York: Wiley, 1974.

Weisz, J. R. Transcontextual validity in developmental research. *Child Development*, 1978, *49*, 1–12.

Author Index